手绘名物系列
Hand-Drawn Classic Travel Landmarks

中国古寺

Ancient Chinese Temples

管维 绘心 文
Written by Guan Wei and Hui Xin

胡亮 译
Translated by Hu Liang

殷鸣 绘
Illustrated by Yin Ming

中国画报出版社·北京
China Pictorial Press · Beijing

图书在版编目（CIP）数据

中国古寺：汉英对照 / 管维, 绘心文；殷鸣绘；
胡亮译. -- 北京：中国画报出版社, 2023.4
（手绘名物系列）
ISBN 978-7-5146-2068-9

Ⅰ.①中… Ⅱ.①管… ②绘… ③殷… ④胡… Ⅲ.
①寺庙—古建筑—介绍—中国—汉、英 Ⅳ.①K928.75

中国版本图书馆CIP数据核字(2022)第039836号

中国古寺（汉英对照）

管维 绘心 文
殷鸣 绘

出 版 人：方允仲
项目主持：方允仲　齐丽华
责任编辑：齐丽华　李聚慧
插画助理：康勇媛　秦　筝
英文翻译：胡　亮
英文编辑：陈星宇
责任印制：焦　洋

出版发行：中国画报出版社
地　　址：中国北京市海淀区车公庄西路33号　邮编：100048
发 行 部：010-88417360　010-68414683（传真）
总编室兼传真：010-88417359　版权部：010-88417359

开　本：16开（787mm×1092mm）
印　张：13.875
字　数：150千字
版　次：2023年4月第1版　2023年4月第1次印刷
印　刷：北京汇瑞嘉合文化发展有限公司
书　号：ISBN 978-7-5146-2068-9
定　价：128.00元

前言

本书是"大美中国"书系中的一本。顾名思义,所谓"大美",无外乎自然界和人类社会中,具有高度审美价值的客体、对象。它们可以是自然界中的山川河流,可以是花鸟虫鱼,也可能是风雨雷电、莺歌燕舞,更有可能是通过色彩、线条、声音、文字等人文艺术表现出来的各种艺术形式,如音乐、舞蹈、建筑、书法、绘画、雕塑、戏剧、电影等。而这些,都来源于东方古老的文明大国——中国。

浑浊而奔腾不息的黄河孕育了古老的华夏文明。中国人的先祖从母亲河走来,由部落壮大成为部落国家,从王国跨越到帝国,经历了漫长的封建时代。最终,在近代的数次实践之后,中国走上了社会主义新中国的道路——在这漫长的历史中,有统一,也有分裂;有强盛,也有衰败。部落演进为国家的历史,中国经历了一千多年,封土建国的周朝,前后存在了八百多年,之后漫长的封建时期,历时两千余年才告结束——可中国的历史,却又不止于长:不仅长,还富于变化。中国五千多年的文明和国家史,从来不是一成不变的:在四千余年的建国史中,中国经历了约十五个朝代,六七十个政权交替更迭,更见证了不计其数的大小战争——战争和政权更替固然给人民带来了深重的灾难,却又在客观上催动着社会生活方方面面的变化,为中国展开了一幅波澜壮阔的历史图卷;从天文、历算到农耕器具的进步,从造纸、印刷到选官制度的变化、商业的繁荣,中华民族就这样一步步走来,走到今天。

Foreword

This book is part of the "Beautiful China" book series. As its name implies, the book series focuses on depicting objects of high aesthetical value in nature and human society. They include not only creatures such as birds, beasts, insects and fish but also natural phenomena such as wind, rain, thunder and lightning. They may also be various forms of art composed with colors, lines, sound and texts, such as music, dance, architecture, calligraphy, painting, sculpture, drama, and movie. Regardless of their form, all of them derive from China, an ancient civilization in the East.

The muddy, ceaseless flow of the Yellow River fostered the ancient Chinese civilization. Nourished by the "mother river", Chinese ancestors gradually developed their tribes into tribal nations, then kingdoms and empires across the feudal era. Eventually, after several attempts of practical exploration in modern times, China embarked on a path of socialism with Chinese characteristics. Throughout its long history, China experienced unifications and separations as well as ups and downs. The history of tribal nations in China lasted for more than 1,000 years, followed by the Zhou dynasty (1046-256 BC) that spanned about 800 years. Then, China entered the feudal period as long as more than 2,000 years. However, the course of China's history is more than just long; it is also full of changes. Across its history of more than 5,000 years, the Chinese civilization has never stopped the pace of evolution. Throughout its history of more than 4,000 years as a nation state, China fostered 15 dynasties and some 70 regimes, and underwent numerous wars. Of course, wars and regime shifts might bring grave disasters to the people, but at the same time they accelerated changes in all aspects of society and composed the eventful picture of Chinese history. From progress in astronomy, calendrical science and farming tools, and improvements in printing and papermaking techniques

前言
Foreword

习近平主席曾多次指出，"当今世界正经历百年未有之大变局"；正是在这样的时代机遇和文化背景下，中国外文局责成中国画报出版社推出了"大美中国"这个书系。本书系既是对中国自然、风物、人文的总结，也是为了向全世界关心中国、热爱中国、崇敬中国的人讲好中国故事。

但凡讲故事，必要有一个主题，有一个入口；我们选择向世界展现中国之美，这并非任意为之。人们总是喜欢美好的东西，这非但是中国人民的追求，也是全世界各国人民、各个民族的追求——不同文化对美的定义或许不同，可这追求却是一致的，而且古来有之。

中国之美既有历史的深邃厚重，又有地域的辽远广阔。大到富丽繁华的都市，小到鲜有问津的村镇，历史总会在这里那里，留下星星点点的痕迹。地域的辽阔又为中国之美赋予了不同的风格。我们既有高山大川，又有小桥流水；既有高屋广厦，又有陋室闲庭；既有"长河落日圆"的雄壮，又有"清泉石上流"的清丽……疆土有多少寸，美就有多少种，简直是说也说不尽的。以自然地理和城镇乡村为依托，我们更想展现一种人文的厚度，南北东西、平原山地、沿海内陆……不同地方的人，

and official selection systems to prosperity of commerce, the Chinese nation have constantly moved forward step by step to the present day.

Chinese President Xi Jinping said on many occasions that the world is undergoing "profound changes unseen in a century." Facing such historic opportunities and cultural context, under the instruction of China International Communications Group, China Pictorial Press presented the "Beautiful China" book series, which not only reviews the natural and cultural sights of China but also tells China's stories to global readers who care, love and admire China.

A story needs a theme or a topic. We do not casually choose "Beautiful China" as the theme of the stories we try to tell. All people love beautiful things. In fact, the pursuit of beauty represents the common aspiration of not only the Chinese people but also people from other parts of the world. The definition of beauty may differ for different cultures, but people around the world have had a shared aspiration for beauty since ancient times.

The beauty of China stems from its profound history and vast territory. Whether in spectacular, prosperous metropolises or in nondescript small towns, we can always find clues left by history. The diverse cultures scattered around the country's vast territory bestow on China different types of beauty. There are high mountains and big rivers as well as exquisite bridges and murmuring streams; there are skyscraping buildings as well as simple dwellings; there are magnificent views of torrential rivers in the setting sun as well as elegant sights of clear streams flowing through rocks… The beauty of China is just as boundless as its territory. With this book, we would like to show readers the natural geography and cultural profundity of various cities, towns and villages across China, from plains to mountains and from coastal areas to inland areas, as well as how people in different regions live in

他们都在以什么样的方式生活着,他们的生活有何不同,而这种种生活又如何共同构成了中国的文化和民生的一部分。一言以蔽之,我们想要传达的,不是某种抽象的概念,不是简单的意象或标准化的符号,而是由真实、具体的细节所构成的鲜活的生活与生命。

本书系通过文图作品讲述中国故事,以画面语言为主,辅以文字的叙述、解释和说明,向读者传递更完善的印象和更系统的知识。

除了摄影作品,我们还将绘画艺术融入到书系当中。例如"手绘名物系列",我们选择了通过水彩画的方式去讲述城市及其民俗的故事,这不仅构成了对城市的刻画,同时也是一次上好的艺术和美学教育。选择水彩画这一既为亚洲也为欧美所熟悉的艺术表现形式,去讲述城市这一最为大多数人所熟悉的生活空间,这是由于我们想以此作为出发点,把中国故事讲好,走近听众,把故事讲得生动真实、可闻可感。

沿着这样的轨迹,我们希望把中国最美的一面展示给世界,也想把中国的故事讲给全世界每一个喜欢她的人听。

different ways and how their lives together compose the country's diverse cultures and lifestyles. In one word, we intend to reveal the vigor of life through true and specific details, rather than an abstract concept, a simple imagery or a standardized symbol.

This book series tells stories about China through vivid pictures and language. Therefore, it prioritizes images, supplemented with textural narrations, explanations and remarks, so as to enable readers to obtain deeper impressions and systematic knowledge.

In addition to photographic works, we also incorporate painting into the book series. For example, the "Hand-Drawn Classic Travel Landmarks" sub-series feature hand-drawn watercolor illustrations depicting cities and their folk customs. This is not only an ideal way to portray cities, but also provides a chance for art and aesthetic education. Watercolor is a form of art familiar to readers around the world. We chose this form of art to portray cities, a kind of living spaces familiar to most people, in an effort to tell China's stories in a vivid, perceptible way and make them closer to readers.

By doing so, we hope to show the most beautiful side of China to the world and tell China's stories to every reader who is interested in the country and its culture.

目录 Contents

前言 Foreword

第一章 Chapter 1
文明互鉴——推动国际交流的寺庙
Mutual Learning between Civilizations——Temples promoting international culture exchange

01 法门寺
　Famen Temple 002

02 东林寺
　Donglin Temple 004

03 南普陀寺
　South Putuo Temple 006

04 大明寺
　Daming Temple 008

05 白马寺
　White Horse Temple 010

06 少林寺
　Shaolin Temple 012

07 隆昌寺
　Longchang Temple 014

08 阿育王寺
　Temple of King Ashoka 016

09 寒山寺
　Hanshan Temple 018

10 正觉寺
　Zhengjue Temple 020

11 开元寺
　Kaiyuan Temple 022

12 龙山寺
　Longshan Temple 024

13 古德寺
　Gude Temple 026

14 净居寺
　Jingju Temple 028

15 冲虚古观
　Chongxu Taoist Temple 030

16 湄洲妈祖庙
　Meizhou Mazu Temple 032

17 三坊七巷天后宫
　　Tianhou Temple at Sanfang Qixiang 034

18 白礁慈济宫
　　Baijiao Ciji Palace 036

19 大雁塔
　　Big Wild Goose Pagoda 038

20 雍和宫
　　Lama Temple 040

第二章 Chapter 2

精绝古艺——艺术史上留名的庙宇
Exquisite Ancient Arts — Temples going down in the history of art

01 隆兴寺
　　Longxing Temple 044

02 柏林禅寺
　　Berlin Zen Temple 046

03 保国寺
　　Baoguo Temple 048

04 佛光寺
　　Foguang Temple 050

05 华严寺
　　Huayan Temple 052

06 智化寺
　　Zhihua Temple 054

07 双林寺
　　Shuanglin Temple 056

08 佛宫寺
　　Buddha Palace Temple 058

09 镇国寺
　　Zhenguo Temple 060

10 法海寺
　　Fahai Temple 062

11 独乐寺
　　Dule Temple 064

12 奉国寺
　　Fengguo Temple 066

13 开元寺
　　Kaiyuan Temple 068

14 光孝寺
　　Guangxiao Temple 070

15 岩山寺
　　Yanshan Temple 072

16 显通寺
　　Xiantong Temple 074

17 崇福寺
　　Chongfu Temple 076

18 安国寺
　　Anguo Temple 078

19 灵山寺
　　Lingshan Temple 080

20 铁佛寺
　　Iron Buddha Temple 082

21 毗卢寺
　　Pilu Temple 084

22 灵岩寺
　　Lingyan Temple 086

23 炳灵寺
　　Bingling Temple 088

24 兴国寺
　　Xingguo Temple 090

25 玉泉寺
　　Yuquan Temple 092

26 天宁禅寺
　　Tianning Temple 094

27 大报恩寺
　　Dabao'en Temple 096

28 文殊院
　　Manjusri Monastery 098

29 罗汉寺
　　Arhat Temple 100

30 灵光寺
　　Lingguang Temple 102

第三章 Chapter 3

觉悟人间——文化史上的名寺
Quest for Spiritual Enlightenment—Famous temples in the history of culture

- 01 栖霞寺
  Qixia Temple 106
- 02 国清寺
  Guoqing Temple 108
- 03 五祖寺
  Wuzu Temple 110
- 04 南华寺
  Nanhua Temple 112
- 05 玄中寺
  Xuanzhong Temple 114
- 06 普救寺
  Pujiu Temple 116
- 07 大相国寺
  Daxiangguo Temple 118
- 08 临济寺
  Linji Temple 120
- 09 麓山寺
  Lushan Temple 122
- 10 开福寺
  Kaifu Temple 124
- 11 归元寺
  Guiyuan Temple 126
- 12 清凉寺
  Qingliang Temple 128
- 13 昭觉寺
  Zhaojue Temple 130

第四章 Chapter 4

溪花禅意——名山胜景中的古寺
Zen in the Spring and Flowers—Ancient temples in famous mountains and scenic spots

01 灵隐寺
　　Lingyin Temple 134

02 天童寺
　　Tiantong Temple 136

03 九华山寺庙群
　　Jiuhua Mountain Temple Complex 138

04 惠山寺
　　Huishan Temple 140

05 悬空寺
　　Hanging Temple 142

06 永祚寺
　　Yongzuo Temple 144

07 塔院寺
　　Tayuan Temple 146

08 外八庙
　　Eight Outer Temples 148

09 天门山寺
　　Tianmenshan Temple 150

10 金山寺
　　Golden Mountain Temple 152

11 镇国寺
　　Zhenguo Temple 154

12 灵岩山寺
　　Lingyanshan Temple 156

13 大召寺
　　Dazhao Temple 158

14 五当召
　　Wudang Lamasery 160

15 布达拉宫
　　Potala Palace 162

16 塔尔寺
　　Ta'er Temple 164

17 拉卜楞寺
　　Labrang Monastery 166

18 仙峰寺
　　Xianfeng Temple 168

19 万年寺
Wannian Temple 170

20 潭柘寺
Tanzhe Temple 172

第五章 Chapter 5

道法自然——著名道观
Following Rules of the Nature——Famous Taoist temples

01 东岳庙
Dongyue Temple 176

02 白云观
Baiyun Taoist Temple 178

03 永乐宫
Yongle Palace 180

04 中岳庙
Zhongyue Temple 182

05 崂山太清宫
Taiqing Palace in Laoshan Mountain 184

06 青羊宫
Qingyang Palace 186

07 紫霄宫
Purple Heaven Palace 188

08 茅山道院
Maoshan Taoist Temple 190

09 抱朴道院
Baopu Taoist Temple 192

10 太和宫
Taihe Palace 194

11 天后宫
Tianhou Temple 196

12 真武阁
Zhenwu Taoist Temple 198

13 泰山岱庙
Taishan Dai Temple 200

14 晋祠
Jinci 202

15 临水宫
Linshui Palace 204

第一章
Chapter I

文明互鉴
Mutual Learning between Civilizations

一 推动国际交流的寺庙
Temples promoting international culture exchange

法门寺
Famen Temple

　　法门寺位于陕西省宝鸡市，因供奉释迦牟尼真身舍利而建塔，因塔而兴寺，其后几百年世人皆以"圣冢"称之。此后的大唐几代君主及勋贵显宦都争相至此瞻礼真身舍利。寺院建筑日益宏伟，通向法门寺的道路上，车马络绎不绝。此时的法门寺塔铃清扬、梵音萦绕，无数稀世之宝被埋入塔下地宫。此种繁华历经几百年有增无减，及至宋代繁盛至极。那时的人们怎么也没想到，此后的千年岁月中三百里秦川依旧，而古寺佛塔在风霜雨雪中颓塌漫漶，尽管屡有修葺，但也无法挽救古塔衰朽的命运。直至20世纪80年代，随着古塔因地震倒塌，法门寺神秘的地宫轰然洞开，从宫廷奇珍到来自东罗马帝国的琉璃器，几千件盛唐珍宝光芒四射，震惊了世界。而那枚舍利子此时已成为世间唯一的释迦牟尼真身舍利、佛教界至高无上的圣物。如今，这枚历经了繁闹与宁静、光明与幽暗的佛祖舍利继续凝聚着世间虔诚的目光，聆听人间百姓的心愿。

　　Famen Temple locates in Baoji, Shaanxi. A pagoda was built in the temple to enshrine the relic of the real body of Sakyamuni, and thus won great popularity for the temple. Over hundreds of years, it was reputed as a "Sacred Tomb". From then on, generations of emperors, high officials and celebrities rushed to pay homage to the relic of the real body of Sakyamuni. Facing a constant stream of visitors, the temple was renovated to become more and more magnificent. At that time, countless rare treasures were stored at its underground palace in the melody of tower bells and chanting of scriptures. Such popularity had lasted for hundreds of years and reached a peak in the Song Dynasty (960–1279). It is beyond the imagination of people at that time that the ancient temple and pagoda suffered from gradual decline in the vicissitudes of the 300-Li Shaanxi region over the following thousands of years. Although they were repaired several times, the fate to decline was not changed. In the 1980s, the ancient pagoda collapsed in an earthquake, revealing the mysterious underground palace of Famen Temple to the public. Thousands of treasures at the heyday of the Tang Dynasty, from rare valuables of the imperial court to colorful glazed glassware of the Eastern Roman Empire, caused a worldwide sensation. Meanwhile, the relic of the real body of Sakyamuni became the only one of its kind as the supreme sacred object in Buddhism. Nowadays, the relic of Sakyamuni, after experiencing bustle and tranquility, was unearthed from darkness to continue to attract the pious sight and listen to the wishes of the people.

02 东林寺
Donglin Temple

东林寺位于江西省九江市庐山西麓，是佛教净土宗发祥地，其法缘远播海内，法脉绵长悠远。东晋高僧慧远因崇尚自然寄情山水，而在庐山修行造寺，同时也开创了名山与古寺的结合，使寺庙不再仅是宗教场所，更成为人们心中远离俗世喧嚣、拥抱自然造化的苑囿园林，后世的"天下名山僧占多"亦由此肇始。自从群山峻岭、山林叠翠间有了这样一座自然清净之所，历代名流高士纷至沓来与东林结缘。谢灵运、陶渊明、孟浩然、韩愈、白居易、柳公权、李邕、王阳明、黄庭坚、周敦颐、王安石、苏东坡、岳飞、陆游……几乎囊尽中国古代所有文豪大家、英雄豪杰。他们在此处观峰林岩洞、瀑布碧潭，留下了许多千古传诵的诗歌笔墨。于是，在美丽的自然景观中，开始有了亭廊桥塔、题刻摩崖等人文景观，最终形成了中国人对名山古迹审美的经典范式。东林已然成为一方净土，可以入梦、入诗、入画……

Located at the western foot of Lushan Mountain in Jiujiang City of Jiangxi Province, Donglin Temple is the birthplace of the Pure Land Sect of Buddhism. With its long history, its influence has spread all over the world. In the Eastern Jin Dynasty (317-420), an eminent monk called Huiyuan built the temple in Lushan as a place of self-cultivation while expressing reverence for nature. He pioneered in building temples on remote mountains, turning temples from a pure religious place into gardens for people to be away from the hustle and bustle of life and embrace the charm of nature. Since then, a lot of temples have been built on famous mountains. After

such a secluded place was constructed on the lush green mountains, celebrities have come one after another to visit it. Xie Lingyun, Tao Yuanming, Meng Haoran, Han Yu, Bai Juyi, Liu Gongquan, Li Yong, Wang Yangming, Huang Tingjian, Zhou Dunyi, Wang Anshi, Su Dongpo, Yue Fei, Lu You ... most of the famous writers and heroes in ancient China had been to the temple. They enjoyed the scenery of peaks, forests, caves, waterfalls, and lakes, and left many famous works that have been passed on to today. Naturally, such cultural landscapes as pavilions, corridors, bridges, towers, and cliffside inscriptions integrated into the beautiful environment become the classic Chinese aesthetic paradigm for famous mountains and historic sites. The pure land of Donglin has become a dreamy, poetic, and picturesque place.

03 南普陀寺
South Putuo Temple

厦门南普陀寺为闽南名刹，居于鹭岛名山五老峰前，背依群峰，面临碧海，古寺建筑依山势而建，中轴线依次层层递高，梵宇琳宫浮现于奇峰碧树云雾缥缈之间，恍若仙境。千年间，古寺香火繁盛、声誉日隆，除了观览名胜的游人信众，更引来许多海外高僧探访。因此，一百年前古寺便建起了佛学院，一度成为海内外佛教交流的中心。海内高僧弘法，十方佛子求经，时至今日，许多国家的高僧大德皆出自学院门下。使南普陀寺扬名海外的不只是佛学，还有素斋。这些历史悠久的素食名菜，口味清纯素雅，制作考究精致。其菜名更充满了佛性与诗意，尤以"半月沉江"这道名菜让人于红尘俗世中品尽禅味。品罢素斋，缓步游至寺院后方，观摩崖石刻，游泉池山景，更可上巅峰亭台，与身后仙山梵宫胜景一同融于海天之间。

Xiamen South Puto Temple is a famous temple in southern Fujian. Surrounded by the blue sea and the Five Old Men Peak, the temple was constructed along the slope of the mountain with one courtyard rising after another on the central axis. Partly hidden in the spectacular peaks, green trees, clouds, and mist, it is like a fairyland. For thousands of years, the ancient temple has been frequented by visitors and won a growing reputation. Apart from tourists and believers, it has attracted many eminent monks from overseas. Therefore, a Buddhist academy was built a century ago, making it a communication center of Buddhist at home and abroad. Till now, eminent monks spread Buddhism and believers from all over the world went on pilgrimage here for Buddhist scriptures. Eminent monks of many countries are disciples of the academy. South Putuo Temple is famous not only for spreading Buddhism but also for vegetarian food. The tasty vegetarian dishes are fastidiously made according to recipes of a long history. Even the name of the dishes is poetic with the rich charm of Buddhism. The famous dish "Half Moon at the River Bottom" provides a glimpse of the Buddhist sense for secular people. After tasting the vegetarian food, visitors can stroll to the back of the temple to enjoy the inscriptions on the cliff and the wonderful mountain scenery. They can also climb up the mountain to have a panoramic view of the holy land of Buddhism between the sea and sky.

04 大明寺
Daming Temple

　　江苏扬州地连吴楚之疆，久称"云水之乡"，自古以来的名贤骚客皆以"烟花三月下扬州"为人生乐事。这座历史文化名城的西北郊，有一座清幽古朴的大明寺。这所千年古寺曾是高僧鉴真东渡日本前，传经授戒之所，因此"山川异域，风月同天"这句曾感动了鉴真并促使其东渡日本的诗句也被刻于寺中供游人信众凭吊。

　　大明寺内不仅有佛家清规戒律，也不乏文人骚客的风流蕴藉。北宋大文学家欧阳修在此筑有"平山堂"，常与友人醉饮千觞，登眺远山，微醺之际挥毫万字；后来苏轼亦在此听牧唱渔歌，赏远树晴川，品"天下第五泉"，为世间留下了脍炙人口的文章佳句。如此美景也引来帝王垂青，清朝几代皇帝都曾为大明寺题联留诗，乾隆皇帝则更是在此寺中修筑御苑，以供游幸。时至今日，古寺风雅未衰，香火炽盛，每日在清脆的梵铃声声中等待着览胜思古的探寻者。

On the border of the ancient states of Wu and Chu, Yangzhou of Jiangsu has long been known as the "Land of Clouds and Waters". Since ancient times, literati and celebrities have taken "a trip to Yangzhou in the mist and flowers of spring" as a great joy in life. On the northwestern outskirts of this historical and cultural city, there is Daming Temple, tranquil and simple. The thousand-year-old temple was the place for Jianzhen to promote Buddhism before he visited Japan. Therefore, the Chinese sentence meaning "lands apart, sky shared" that touched Jianzhen and prompted him to travel eastward to Japan was inscribed in the temple for visitors to commemorate him.

Daming Temple is not only a site of Buddhism but also a place to show the charm of the literati. Ouyang Xiu, a great writer of the Northern Song Dynasty (960–1127), built the "Pingshan Hall" in the temple. He often drank and chat merrily with his friends. Looking at the distant mountains, he wrote many wonderful articles when he was slightly drunk. Later, Su Shi frequented the hall to listen to the fishermen's song, to enjoy the picturesque scenery, and to taste "the fifth spring in the world", leaving numerous famous articles and famous sentences. The beautiful scenery also attracted the attention of emperors. Several emperors of the Qing Dynasty (1636-1912) wrote couplets and poems for the temple. Emperor Qianlong even built an imperial garden in the temple for pleasure. Today, the ancient temple remains its elegance and influence, waiting for visitors to view the scenery and reflect the history in the crisp sound of Buddhist bells.

白马寺
White Horse Temple

东汉永平年间,天竺白马驮经入洛阳,"白马寺"始创,此后佛教寺院中的"寺"字便应运而生。三千繁华,弹指刹那,今日的白马寺已成中国佛教的"祖庭"与"释源",引来了八方多国高僧大德与信众来此,遂成就了世间唯一一座拥有中、印、缅、泰四国风格佛殿的寺院,从不辜负"天下第一寺"的盛名。大千世界,战火离乱,白马寺几度废兴、几度重修。佛堂幽寂禅声动,菩提依旧了无尘。白马寺的梵语、钟声仍在岁月中悠扬,红墙黛瓦,高塔齐云,庄严肃穆。

During the Yongping period of the Eastern Han Dynasty (25-220), monks from India used white horses to carry Buddhist scriptures to Luoyang. The White Horse Temple was founded. Later, the Chinese character "si" was widely used in the name of temples. The past glory faded in the flying time. The White Horse Temple has now been viewed as "the cradle of Chinese Buddhism", attracting many eminent monks or believers from different countries. As a result, it was turned into the only temple with Chinese, Indian, Myanmarese, and Thailand-style Buddhist halls to live up to the reputation of "the most famous temple". In the war fire and vicissitudes of times, the White Horse Temple had been abandoned and rebuilt several times. Nowadays, chanting of scriptures and ringing of bells are still heard in the solemn and tranquil temple with red walls, green tiles, and rising towers.

06 少林寺
Shaolin Temple

少林寺，既是中国佛教禅宗祖庭又是中国功夫的发源地，因古寺位于河南嵩山腹地少室山茂林之中，故名"少林寺"。这座古寺在世俗世界中的响亮标签甚多，无论是"世界文化遗产"，还是"全国重点文物保护单位"，都敌不过"功夫"二字对世界的震撼。全世界无数热爱功夫的"朝圣者"纷纷来此"朝觐"，津津乐道于千年间少林寺的功夫在政治权力、家国情仇间交织的奇闻异事，竟都忘却了这里也是佛教禅宗的发祥地，也曾有达摩一苇渡江的传奇故事。也许正因为与世俗更加接近，少林寺逐渐变成了一个醒目的东方文化符号，即使我们身在异国他乡，也能感受到这个醒目符号所代表的骄傲和家国情怀。亲赴少林寺，在了却一睹"功夫"真容的夙愿之后，也能于青灯古佛旁感受心境的安然与清静，此时手中那一炷清香所承载的不再是世俗欲望，而是精神寄托。

Shaolin Temple is recognized as the birthplace of Chan Buddhism and the cradle of Shaolin Kung Fu. The name reflects its location in the ancient grove of Mount Shaoshi, in the hinterland of Songshan mountains. This ancient temple has many resounding labels in the secular world. Neither the title of "World Cultural Heritage" nor "National Key Cultural Relic Protection Unit" could parallel its influence through "Kung Fu" on the world. Countless "pilgrims" who love Kung Fu crowded to the temple. Talking about the stories of Kung Fu in political power, family and national conflicts, and so on, over thousands of years; they forgot that it was the birthplace of Chan Buddhism with the legend of Bodhidharma crossing the river on a reed. Perhaps the proximity to the secular world has gradually turned the Shaolin Temple into an eye-catching symbol of Eastern culture. Even those living in a foreign country can feel the pride and patriotism represented by it. I hope that I can go to Shaolin Temple in person not only to realize the long-cherished dream to watch the true "Kung Fu" but also to feel the peace and tranquility of my inner world besides the ancient Buddha and oil lamp. At that time, the incense in my hand expresses no longer the secular desire but my spiritual comfort.

隆昌寺
Longchang Temple

　　江苏句容的宝华山风景秀美，游玩时可见一座座马头墙相连，一片片浓郁的徽派建筑迎面而来，这便是静卧于山中的隆昌寺。一扇极其窄小的山门后藏着气派恢宏的明代建筑群，一道道幽深的蜿蜒回廊将你带进一重重院落之中，高低起伏的窄道台阶似乎总在眼前绵延无尽。此地有着"律宗第一名山"之称，无论是飞檐斗拱的建筑，还是精致华丽的砖雕彩画，都彰显着佛教律宗发祥地的气派。始建者宝志禅师相传为中国民间传说中济公的原型。隆昌寺佛事昌隆，更以受戒闻名天下，甚至日本、泰国、缅甸、印度等国亦有僧尼不远万里来此受戒。

　　隆昌古寺的声望和美景赢得帝王也频频垂青，其中乾隆皇帝六下江南都曾临幸于此。如今，天下王朝几番兴废，帝王往事无可追忆，唯有寺中古老的无梁铜殿在华山律腔的千古梵音中看尽世间枯荣。

At the picturesque Baohua Mountain in Jurong of Jiangsu, visitors could see rows of Hui-style architecture with horse-head walls and it is the Longchang Temple. Magnificent buildings of the Ming Dynasty hide behind an extremely narrow gate. Long winding corridors lead to one courtyard after another and it seems that the undulating narrow stairs are endless. Reputed as the "No.1 Mountain of Vinaya School", both the architecture with overhanging eaves and brackets and the exquisite brick carvings and colorful paintings show the style of the cradle of Vinaya School of Chinese Buddhism. The temple was originally built by monk Baozhi, the prototype of Ji Gong in Chinese folklore. The thriving temple is famous for its initiation into monkhood, so even believers from other countries, including Japan, Thailand, Myanmar and India traveled thousands of miles for this purpose.

The prestige and beautiful scenery of the Longchang Temple have drawn the attention of emperors. Emperor Qianlong had been to the temple each time during his six visits to the Yangtze River Delta. Nowadays, the past stories of emperors could hardly be remembered with the rise and fall of dynasties, leaving only the ancient beamless copper hall there in the chanting of Buddhist scriptures.

08 阿育王寺
Temple of King Ashoka

东越胜境的宁波自古就有"东南佛国"之美誉，以其山明水秀，引来高僧大德在此修筑了几多名刹庵宇。其中，阿育王寺以珍藏佛国珍宝释迦牟尼的真身舍利及玲珑精致的舍利宝塔而闻名中外。古寺环山面水，一派远离尘世之象，寺内不仅有重檐歇山、翘角飞檐的华丽殿堂，也有玲珑精致的元代古塔。千年来，寺内高僧多饱学之士，使得古寺禅韵悠远，法脉绵长，不但吸引了诸如苏轼等文豪名士，更是影响到了中国周边的国家。许多日本古代名画中亦可见到阿育王寺中的舍利宝塔。但古老的阿育王寺并没有尘封在古书经卷、丹青名画之中，而是佛事日隆，法会不断，钟磬鱼鼓与诵经声时常回荡于千年古殿，为芸芸众生祈祷着身心安乐。

Reputed as the "Buddhist Kingdom in the Southeast", Ningbo has attracted eminent monks to build many famous temples with its beautiful natural scenery. Among them, the Temple of King Ashoka is famous all around the world for its collection of the relic of the real body of Sakyamuni and the exquisite pagoda to contain it. Facing a lake, the ancient temple is suited in the remote mountain area. There are not only magnificent halls with hip-and-gable roofs and double upturned eaves but also exquisite ancient towers constructed in the Yuan Dynasty (1271–1368). For thousands of years, eminent monks in the temple are mostly men of great learning, which has attracted many learned literati like Su Shi and increased its far-reaching influence on Buddhism to the neighboring countries of China. The pagoda to contain the relic of the real body of Sakyamuni in the Temple of King Ashoka could also be found in many famous ancient Japanese paintings. Nevertheless, the ancient Temple of King Ashoka is not excluded from the world by the ancient books, Buddhist scriptures, and famous paintings. Buddhist ceremonies and rites are frequently held in the temple to pray for the well-being of all living beings with the resounding sound of bells and wooden fish as well as the reciting of scriptures.

09 寒山寺
Hanshan Temple

寒山寺始建于南朝。寺内古迹遗存甚多,尤以诗文碑刻甚佳。寒山寺因唐代诗僧寒山而得名。他的诗歌通过挚友僧人拾得传遍了日本,寒山那豁达、透彻的人生感悟影响了此后日本文化上千年。而千年之后,这些诗歌又从日本传遍了20世纪50年代的美国,颓狂的山之隐者——寒山,变成了那一代美国青年心中反主流文化的先锋。查尔斯·弗雷泽的著名小说《寒山》,在扉页上赫然写着寒山的一句诗——"人问寒山道,寒山路不通"。彼时万里之遥的中国,古老的寒山寺正安然静卧于姑苏古城,用它那直入人心的钟声传递着穿越历史、国家和语言的诗性光辉。

Hanshan Temple was built in the Southern dynasties. Among numerous relics in the temple, poems and stone stele inscriptions are especially good. The name of the temple derives from Hanshan, a legendary monk and poet in the Tang Dynasty. His poems were spread throughout Japan by his close friend monk Shide and influenced Japanese culture for thousands of years with his open-minded and thorough understanding of life. Thousands of years later, these poems were spread from Japan to the United States in the 1950s. Hanshan, the pioneering hermit, became the vanguard of counterculture in the mind of a generation of American youth. In his famous novel *Cold Mountain*, Charles Frazier quoted the poem by Hanshan at a glaring place on the title page, "Men ask the way to Cold Mountain, and there's no way through." Thousands of miles away in China, the ancient Hanshan Temple is suited in Suzhou City, passing its poetic glory transcending history, country, and language with the penetrating sound of bells.

正觉寺
Zhengjue Temple

　　正觉寺坐落于吉林敦化,是始建于清光绪年间的东北古刹。寺中皆是出家修行的比丘尼。古寺原本香火鼎盛,但"二战"的兵火涂炭让古寺中的比丘尼四方离散,辉煌不再。但离散于乱世的比丘尼形散而神聚,人离古寺而佛存心中。20世纪70年代,一位漂泊至美国多年的正觉寺法师在纽约修建了正觉寺下院,向世人弘扬佛法和中华文化。此后的几十年中,她云游各国,一直为重修敦化正觉寺正院呕心沥血。在她的不懈努力下,20世纪90年代,敦化正觉寺终于法脉重延,恢复了袅袅香火。如今的正觉寺已经是举世闻名的亚洲最大的尼众道场。古寺依山傍水,山林叠翠,在白山黑水间重新响起悠悠梵音。

Located in Dunhua of Jilin Province, Zhengjue Temple is an ancient temple in northeast China constructed during the reign of Emperor Guangxu in the Qing Dynasty. It is a temple for the self-cultivation of Bhikkhunis. It had attracted an endless stream of pilgrims, yet the Bhikkhunis as well as the past glory of the temple were driven away in the gun fire of World War II. Although they left the temple in troubled times, their belief in Buddhism never changed. In the 1970s, a Bhikkhuni who had been in the United States for many years after leaving the Zhengjue Temple built a branch of Zhengjue Temple in New York to promote Buddhism and Chinese culture. In the following decades, she traveled all over the world and made every endeavor to the rebuilding of Zhengjue Temple in Dunhua. Owning to her unremitting efforts, it was rebuilt and opened to the public in the 1990s. Nowadays, Zhengjue Temple has recovered its status as the largest and most famous temple for the self-cultivation of Bhikkhunis. The chanting of scriptures is resounding again in the temple surrounded by verdant forests, mountains, and rivers in northeast China.

开元寺
Kaiyuan Temple

　　开元寺位于中国古代"海上丝绸之路"的重要起点泉州，始建于唐垂拱二年（686）。到了宋代，随着泉州港的繁盛，所有通过海路造访中国的外国人在登陆上岸前，最先遥望到的中华风物便是寺中巍峨耸立的东西双塔了。泉州曾经中外贸易文化交流频繁昌盛，使得这座古寺有着世界多种文明的痕迹。大殿后廊的檐柱上雕刻着印度教神话故事，而月台须弥座的束腰上却装饰着浓厚古希腊风格的人面狮身图案。殿内柱和桁梁接合处的木雕斗拱并非常见的瑞兽，而是二十四尊飞天乐伎人像，这些雕像斗拱融敦煌飞天、印度妙音鸟、欧洲安琪儿等造型艺术为一体，为世界木构建筑所罕见。开元寺以其宏伟的外形和丰富的内涵展示了"海上丝绸之路"的灿烂文明和中华文化的包容性、多元性。

Originally built in the second year of the reign of Emperor Chuigong in the Tang Dynasty (686), Kaiyuan Temple is located in Quanzhou, the important starting point of the ancient Maritime Silk Road. The Song Dynasty witnessed the flourishing of the Quanzhou Port. All foreigners visiting China by sea would see two rising towers in the temple in the distance before their landing. With frequent and prosperous trade and culture exchange between China and foreign countries, the temple was left with traces of various civilizations worldwide. Stories of Indian mythology are carved on the pillars of the back porch of the main hall, while the suyao of the Sumeru base on the terrace is decorated with the pattern of the sphinx in ancient Greek style. On the bracket set at the junction of the pillars and truss beams, it is not a common auspicious beast but 24 musicians Gandhanra integrating the plastic arts of Dunhuang Gandhanra, Indian Kalaviuka, and European angels, which is rare in wooden architecture worldwide. With its magnificent design and rich connotation, Kaiyuan Temple demonstrates the splendid civilization of the Maritime Silk Road and the inclusiveness and diversity of Chinese culture.

龙山寺
Longshan Temple

　　安海龙山寺以规模宏伟、布局严整、结构奇妙和巧夺天工的雕刻艺术而名噪海内外，几经废兴，现存典型的清代闽南传统寺宇建筑。寺院重檐起翘，随处可见木雕、石雕，代表了明清时期闽南建筑的营造工艺和雕刻工艺水平。其中，千手千眼观音立像、传世大鼓、金刚殿两扇整版樟木门，皆由整木（樟木）做成，因此有传言它们出自同一千年古樟，被称为"樟树三宝"。

　　古寺历时千余年，传布广远。清乾隆年间，因福建晋江与台湾鹿港通航，两岸贸易兴盛，龙山寺的香火随即传至台湾，仅台湾一岛就有几百座寺宇都以"龙山寺"为名，其中最著名的是鹿港龙山寺和台北艋舺龙山寺。此外，国外远至东南亚、美洲诸国亦有许多"龙山寺"。而安海龙山寺作为天下龙山寺的祖庭，既见证了两岸信俗一脉相承，也将圆融智慧传播世界。

Located in the Anhai town of Jinjiang, Longshan Temple is renowned worldwide for its magnificent scale, rigorous layout, exquisite structure, and ingenious carving art. After experiencing ups and downs, it now features typical traditional temple buildings constructed in the Qing Dynasty in southern Fujian. The architecture is of the upturned double eave. Wood carvings and stone carvings representing the construction and carving craftsmanship of southern Fujian in the Ming and Qing dynasties could be frequently seen in the temple. Among them, the statue of Avalokitesvara Bodhisattva, the big drum, and the gate of the Vajra Hall are made of whole wood (from the camphor tree). Legend has it that they are made of the wood from the same thousand-year-old camphor three, so they are called "Three Camphor Treasures."

The thousand years old temple has widespread influence. During the reign of Emperor Qianlong in the Qing Dynasty, Jinjiang of Fujian and Lukang of Taiwan established shipping connections and cross-strait trade was flourishing. The influence of the temple spread to Taiwan with hundreds of temple buildings in the island of Taiwan named after Longshan. The most famous two are Lukang Longshan Temple and Taipei Bangka Longshan Temple. Besides, there are many Longshan Temples abroad in Southeast Asia and America. As the birthplace of Longshan Temple, Anhai Longshan Temple not only witnessed the passing down of Buddhism across the strait but also spread the wisdom of harmony to the world.

古德寺
Gude Temple

在湖北武汉市汉口黄浦路上，一片鳞次栉比的现代建筑中，隐藏着一处有百年历史的佛教寺院——古德寺。它始建于清晚期，初建时仿缅甸"阿难陀寺"式风格，是一座融东西方特色于一体的建筑。随着武昌起义的爆发，武汉这座传奇城市涌入了大量西方文化艺术，而古德寺也在此后屡次的扩建中融合了多种异域文化的鲜明特点。古德寺的这种多文明融合特色生动地体现了时代与文化变革对古老佛教的影响，以及与中国传统文化的融会贯通。

古德寺主体建筑群和传统的中国寺庙建筑一样，由山门、天王殿、大雄宝殿（圆通宝殿）、观音堂、藏经楼等组成，但核心建筑圆通宝殿却是西方哥特式古典建筑风格。古德寺的建筑融合了东西方多种文化的视觉元素，是中国传统文化与西方文化碰撞交流的产物。或许佛教圆融的本质成就了这座风格奇特的古寺，也或许是近百年来变革激荡的人文思潮造就了它。今天的古德寺，作为藏身于闹市中的清修之所，依旧传出声声悠长的梵音。

Among rows of modern buildings on Huangpu Road at Hankou in Wuhan of Hubei Province, there is a Buddhist temple of a hundred years old called Gude Temple. It was built in the late Qing Dynasty. Following the style of the Ananda Temple of Myanmar, it is a building that combines Eastern and Western characteristics. With the outbreak of the Wuchang Uprising, western culture and art flooded into the legendary city of Wuhan which added a variety of exotic cultures in the expansions of Gude Temple. The merge of different civilizations in Gude Temple vividly reflects the influence of political revolution and culture reform on ancient Buddhism and the final integration into the traditional Chinese culture.

Like other Chinese temples, the main building complex of the Gude Temple is comprised of the Mountain Gate, Hall of Heavenly Kings, Mahavira Hall (Yuantong Hall), Guanyin Hall, and Scripture Room. Nevertheless, as the main hall, the Yuantong Hall is of classical western Gothic style. Covering visual elements of multiple cultures from both the East and the West, the architecture of Gude Temple is the product of the exchange between Chinese traditional culture and western culture. Perhaps the temple with a peculiar style comes either from the inclusiveness of Buddhism or the turbulent trend of humanistic thought in the past century. The chanting of scriptures could still be heard in the tranquil temple hidden in the hustle and bustle of the city.

净居寺
Jingju Temple

净居寺始建于唐朝，史载鉴真和尚第五次东渡日本时因海风受阻，中途折回，曾居于此。宋代，以热爱艺术著称的宋徽宗赵佶改赐此寺为"净居寺"，遂以此名闻达于世。

净居寺所在青原山飞瀑流泉，茂林叠翠。古寺虽然法脉绵延久远，但更以文脉昌明著称于世。寺内曾设青原书院，历代大儒名士如颜真卿、文天祥、黄庭坚等都曾至此览胜，留下墨迹。明代思想家王阳明将青原书院改为阳明学院，并迁至寺旁。于是几百年来，朗朗的读书声与悠扬的梵铃声朝夕相伴，阳明心学与佛教禅宗相对而望，这或许是世人总有以"禅骨儒表""类禅"来评价"心学"的一个原因。"二战"时期，本地国立中学迁至净居寺内，千年古寺再次传来清朗的读书声，中华少年在烽烟乱世中以强大的定力勤奋学习。如今的净居寺依旧有着超绝于尘世的清净，香烟袅袅，晨钟暮鼓，多了几分清凉与适意。

Jingju Temple was built in the Tang Dynasty. According to historical records, monk Jianzhen had lived here when obstructed by the bad weather on the sea and turned back halfway during his fifth trip to Japan. In the Song Dynasty, Emperor Huizong Zhao Ji, who was famous for his passion for art, named the temple "Jingju Temple" and the name was used since then.

Jingju Temple is located in Qingyuan Mountain with springs, waterfalls, and flourishing forests. Despite its far-reaching influence on Buddhism, the temple is more famous for its position in literature and culture. Qingyuan Academy was established in the temple and famous scholars in previous dynasties, like Yan Zhenqing, Wen Tianxiang, Huang Tingjian, had visited the temple and left their writings. Wang Yangming, the thinker of the Ming Dynasty (1368–1644), changed Qingyuan Academy to Yangming Academy and moved it next to the temple. Therefore, the voice of reading has been accompanied by the melody of the bells in the temple for hundreds of years. The philosophy of the mind by Wang Yangming echoes with Chan Buddhism, which perhaps could explain the inner connection between the Mind Confucianism and Buddhism as put forward by many people. During World War II, a local national middle school moved into Jingju Temple. The clear voice of reading was heard in the thousand-year-old temple once again. Chinese teenagers studied diligently with strong determination in the turmoil of the war. In the curling upward smoke of incense and the sounds of bell and drums, the Jingju Temple is now still a secluded land of tranquility and comfort.

 冲虚古观
Chongxu Taoist Temple

　　冲虚古观位于广东惠州罗浮山。此处雄峙岭南、坐临南海,山中飞瀑名泉众多,古木繁茂天然,是一处远离俗世、清净修行之地。东晋时,道教传奇人物葛洪在此炼丹修行,修建了炼丹南庵,宋代帝王御赐此观为"冲虚观"。据史载,历代帝王求雨也多在古观设有祭坛。

　　古观屡有废兴,历代均有修葺,现存建筑为清代重修,因此为四合院式庭院建筑。冲虚古观靠山面水,观前湖水清澈,水中倒影与岸上古老的建筑虚实相生,使人未进观心便澄明安静起来。抬首仰望,各殿之上覆以色泽耀目的琉璃瓦,正脊是灵动逼真的大型彩色陶塑,其余各处也满是雕镂华丽的金漆浮雕木构件。古观内的三清宝殿左侧有葛仙祠,右侧有黄大仙祠,因此,海内外许多道观如香港黄大仙、马来西亚和新加坡的黄龙庙皆以其为发祥地。

Chongxu Taoist Temple is located in Luofu Mountain of Huizhou in Guangdong province. Facing the South China Sea, the temple located in the Lingnan mountains with famous waterfalls and springs and luxuriant ancient trees is a secluded place for self-cultivation. In the Eastern Jin Dynasty (317-420), the Taoist legend Ge Hong made pills of immorality and conducted spiritual practice here and built Liandannan Temple. In the Song Dynasty, the temple was named by the emperor "Chongxu Temple." According to historical records, many emperors in past dynasties had set up altars in the temple to pray for rain.

In its rises and falls, the temple had been repaired in the past dynasties. The current courtyard-style buildings were constructed in the Qing Dynasty. Backed by the mountains, the temple faces a lake. The reflection of the ancient buildings in the crystal-clear water makes the reality interwoven with the empty, helping visitors to seek their inner peace before they enter the temple. Looking up, the halls are covered with dazzling glazed tiles. The main ridge is a vivid colored pottery sculpture. Gold lacquer relief inscription could be frequently seen in the temple. The main hall, Sanqing Hall, is flanked by Gexian Hall on the left and Huangdaxian Hall on the right. Therefore, it was considered as the birthplace of many Taoist temples at home and abroad, like Huangdaxian Temple in Hong Kong, Huanglong Temples in Malaysia and Singapore, and so on.

湄洲妈祖庙
Meizhou Mazu Temple

　　妈祖最早是沿海渔民的保护神，后来随着"海上丝绸之路"的贸易往来、文化交流，妈祖信仰遍布世界几十个国家，全球信众近三亿人。湄洲妈祖庙位于福建省莆田市湄洲岛，是妈祖文化的起源地，是全球妈祖信仰的祖庙，也是信众的朝圣中心。晴日，游人信众乘船欲往，未登岛时，便可在海上望到金碧辉煌的琳宫，以及山顶慈穆庄严的妈祖圣像。

　　古庙始建于北宋，历代皆有扩建。湄洲岛上依山凿石筑起层级递进的重重楼台殿宇，古庙山顶还建有巨型妈祖石雕像。在岛上绵延几十千米的海岸线上，巍峨壮观的妈祖庙面朝碧海金沙，背靠青山翠林，游人信众由山门拾级而上，沿途馆殿楼阁连缀不断，回望身后千帆聚集，水天一色，更觉身入龙宫仙境。

　　Mazu is originally considered the protector of fishermen in coastal areas. With the development of the ancient Maritime Silk Road and cultural exchanges, the Mazu belief and custom have been spread to dozens of countries with nearly 300 million followers. Meizhou Mazu Temple is located on Meizhou Island in Putian City of Fujian Province. As the cradle of Mazu culture, it is the ancestor Temple of Mazu belief worldwide and the pilgrimage center. On a sunny day, visitors and pilgrims could see the magnificent Lin Palace and the majestic statue of Mazu on the top of the mountain on the boat before they arrived at the island.

The temple was built in the Northern Song dynasty and expanded in the following dynasties. One courtyard after another has been constructed along the slope of the mountain on the Meizhou island. There is also a giant stone statue of Mazu on the top of the mountain temple. Backed by the lush green mountainous in an island with a coastline of dozens of kilometers, the magnificent Mazu Temple faces the blue ocean. When visitors and pilgrims go up along the steps connecting the halls and pavilions, the wonderful ocean scenery would make them feel that they are visiting the dragon palace.

17 三坊七巷天后宫
Tianhou Temple at Sanfang Qixiang

福州古城中的三坊七巷是自晋、唐起形成的贵族和士大夫的聚居地，名人旧宅故居比屋连甍。在这片风格婉约别致的建筑群中，沿着古老的青石板路走至郎官巷，远远可见一扇朱漆大门，那便是天后宫了。进门后依次是前殿、正殿和后殿。前殿有戏台，院内石板铺地，两侧建有厢廊。正殿顶部有鎏金藻井，华丽精巧，七层如意斗拱叠层盘旋结顶。殿正中的妈祖神像优美华贵，天师、财神、天尊等则供奉在后殿，一派道教风貌。

天后妈祖一直是沿海水路发达地区人民的传统信仰，于是天后宫也逐渐成了三坊七巷古城居民的公共空间，既有根植于信仰的礼斗祈福、福船开光、迎财神，也有里巷人家、榕城居民的各类文化娱乐活动。逢年过节时，前殿戏台每每响起悠扬婉转的闽剧，两廊观者如云，此间一砖一瓦，一树一花，伴着耳畔闽韵榕腔仿佛穿越了时光。

Sanfang Qixiang, literally Three Lanes and Seven Alleys, is a historic and cultural area in the city of Fuzhou. Aristocrats and scholar-officials have lived in the area since the Jin and Tang dynasties, so former residences of many celebrities could be found here. In the graceful and exquisite architectural complex, a red lacquered gate can be seen at Langguan Lane when visitors walk along the ancient stone road. It is Tianhou Temple. After entering the gate, visitors will pass the front hall, the main hall, and the back hall in order. In the stone slabs paved courtyard at the front hall, there is a stage and porches on both sides. On the roof of the main hall, there is a splendid gilt caisson of a seven-cross bracket set. The Mazu statue in the center is beautiful and elegant. The Celestial Master, God of Wealth and Celestial Venerable are enshrined in the back hall, showing a typical layout of Taoism temples.

Tianhou Mazu has always been the traditional belief of the people in coastal regions. As a result, Tianhou Temple gradually entered the public space for residents of Sanfang Qixiang to hold not only ceremonies to pray for happiness, bless for protection over ships, and welcome the god of wealth but also a diversity of entertainment activities. During the holidays and festivals, the melodious Fujian Opera would be performed on the stage at the front hall, bringing spectators back into their memories with everything around them.

白礁慈济宫
Baijiao Ciji Temple

　　白礁慈济宫位于福建省漳州龙海市角美镇白礁村，是奉祀医神保生大帝的祖宫。自南宋肇建以来，白礁慈济宫便以其巍峨的宫殿式建筑、精美的艺术装饰，被誉为"闽南故宫"。慈济宫是一座五门三进宫殿式建筑，分前中后三殿，前殿两边如同皇宫一般设有文武朝房，这在中国古代寺庙建筑中极为少见。慈济宫中仍可见到石雕等南宋遗珍，殿宇之中梁栋雕饰极尽华美精致。每逢各类隆重的祭祀活动，虔诚信众便从四方赶来。

　　慈济宫宏大华丽，是闽台地区历史与文化传承的载体。东南沿海地区，人们对保生大帝的信仰由来已久，慈济宫作为发祥地，千年来香火绵延，祭祀不绝。随着此地的人民漂洋出海，保生大帝的信仰传遍东南亚。因闽台之间人员船只来往频繁，白礁慈济宫在台湾还拥有三百多间分灵宫庙。慈济宫不仅传承了信仰，也传承了文化与艺术，并将这些融入社会文化活动中，成为闽南地区独有的人文景观。

Located in Baijiao Village of Jiaomei Town in Zhangzhou City of Fujian Province, Baijiao Ciji Temple is the center for worshiping Baosheng Emperor, a Chinese god of medicine. Since its establishment in the Southern Song Dynasty, the temple has been known as the "Imperial Palace of Southern Fujian" for its magnificent palace-style architecture and exquisite artistic decoration. It is a five-bay wide and three-bay deep palace-style building. There are three halls. The front hall is flanked by rooms on both sides like the imperial palace, which is rare in architecture for temples in ancient China. Stone carvings and other relics of the Southern Song Dynasty can still be found in the temple. The decorations in the halls are extremely beautiful and exquisite. On occasions of grand sacrificial activities, pious believers gather here from all directions.

The grand and magnificent Ciji Temple is a reflection of the historical and cultural inheritance of Fujian and Taiwan. In the southeast coastal areas, the belief in Baosheng Emperor can be traced back to ancient times. As the ancestral temple of the belief, it has been frequented by endless pilgrims and visitors for thousands of years. With the frequent exchange between Fujian and Taiwan, over 300 branches of the temple have been established in Taiwan. The belief has also been spread abroad to Southeast Asia. Ciji Temple spreads not only the belief but also culture and art. Moreover, they are integrated into social and cultural activities to form a unique cultural landscape in southern Fujian.

大雁塔
Big Wild Goose Pagoda

　　大雁塔因"雁塔题名"和"雁塔诗会",在中国文化史上留下了重要一笔。同时它还因玄奘法师西天取经、弘扬佛法的传奇故事闻名天下。

　　大雁塔位于陕西省西安市南的大慈恩寺内,又名"慈恩寺塔"。它是现存最早、规模最大的唐代四方楼阁式砖塔,是古印度佛寺的建筑形式与华夏文化融合的典型建筑,并保存了大量精美的线刻画及砖雕对联。据传,唐代画家吴道子、文学家王维也曾在此画过壁画。在大雁塔底层南门洞两侧镶嵌着"二圣三绝碑"——《大唐三藏圣教序》碑和《大唐三藏圣教序记》碑,这两座碑分别由唐太宗李世民、唐高宗李治撰文,皆由大书法家褚遂良手书,是研究唐代书法、雕刻艺术的重要文物。

　　千百年来,大雁塔不仅有杜甫、岑参、高适、白居易、储光羲等文人的吟诗作对,还镌刻了丝绸之路上佛教传播的历史。

Big Wild Goose Pagoda has played an important role in the history of Chinese culture due to the stories of "inscription of the name of who passed the imperial exam" and "meeting of five great poets". Meanwhile, it is also famous for the legends of the journey to the west by Master Xuanzang.

Located in the Daci'en Temple in the south of Xi'an of Shaanxi Province, the Big Wild Goose Pagoda is also known as the "Pagoda of Ci'en Temple". It is the earliest and largest existing quartet attic style brick tower of the Tang Dynasty. It is a typical building for the integration of the architectural form of ancient Indian Buddhist temples with Chinese culture. A lot of exquisite line carvings and brick couplets have been well-preserved. According to legend, the famous painter Wu Daozi and the famous writer Wang Wei also created murals here. The two sides of the south entrance at the bottom level of the Big Wild Goose Pagoda are inlaid with two stone tablets inscribed the passage drafted by Emperor Taizong of Tang Dynasty Li Shimin and Emperor Gaozong of Tang Dynasty Li Zhi respectively and written by the great calligrapher Chu Suiliang. They are important cultural relics for studying calligraphy and carving art in the Tang Dynasty.

The Big Wild Goose Pagoda has not only attracted famous poets such as Du Fu, Cen Shen, Gao Shi, Bai Juyi, and Chu Guangxi to compose verses but also engraved the history of spreading Buddhism along the Silk Road over thousands of years.

20 雍和宫
Lama Lamasery

  雍和宫位于北京市，其前身是康熙皇帝赐给四儿子胤禛的府邸，即后来的雍亲王府。又因乾隆皇帝诞生于此，雍和宫出了两位皇帝——雍正皇帝和乾隆皇帝，便有了"龙潜福地"之称。因此，雍和宫黄瓦红墙，与紫禁城皇宫同等规格，尽显皇家气势。乾隆九年（1744），雍和宫被改为喇嘛庙，成了清朝中后期全国规格最高的一座佛教寺院。

  雍和宫主要由三座精致的牌坊和五进宏伟的大殿组成，从飞檐斗拱的东西牌坊到古色古香的东、西顺山楼，有千余间殿宇。行走其间，扑面而来的是大气宏伟的气息，目及所处皆是融汉、满、蒙等各民族建筑艺术于一体的风格独特的建筑。雍和宫主殿内供奉着三世佛像，左为过去世燃灯佛，中为现在世释迦牟尼佛，右为未来世弥勒佛，表示过去、现在和未来无时不有佛。游人观之，顿感时空浩瀚，人如尘埃，贪嗔痴皆是庸人自扰。

    Located in Beijing, Lama Lamasery is previously the residence of Yinzhen, the fourth son of Emperor Kangxi, namely "Prince Yong's Mansion". As Emperor Qianlong was born here, it was the former residence of two emperors, Emperor Yongzheng and Emperor Qianlong, so it was called an "imperial blessed land". Therefore, the architecture adopted the same standard as that of the Forbidden City with the imperial yellow tiles and red walls. In the 9th year of the reign of Emperor Qianlong (1744), it was changed into a lamasery, becoming the Buddhist temple of the highest standard all over the country in the mid and late Qing Dynasty.

    It is composed of three exquisite archways and five magnificent main halls. From the memorial archway with overhanging eaves and brackets to the antique east and west gates, there are thousands of rooms. Magnificence dominates the whole atmosphere with architecture integrating the art of various ethnic groups like Han, Manchu, and Mongolian. The main hall houses statues of Three Ages of Buddhas, with the statue of Gautama Buddha in the center, which is flanked by the statue of Dīpankara Buddha on the right and the Maitreya Buddha on the left, indicating that there are always Buddhas in the past, present, and future. Visitors would feel that humanity is so tiny in the boundless universe and desire, anger, and ignorance are unnecessary fuss made by the simple-minded people.

第二章
Chapter 2

精绝古艺
Exquisite Ancient Arts

一 艺术史上留名的庙宇
Temples going down in the history of art

01 隆兴寺
Longxing Temple

　　正定古城一隅藏有一座中华名刹，此处原是皇家御苑，隋文帝时在苑内改建寺院，时称龙藏寺，后世扩建时改为隆兴寺。寺内颇多唐宋遗迹，无论建筑、雕塑、壁画、碑刻均为传世至宝。因此，隆兴寺备受历代帝王青睐，千百年间纷纷来此巡行驻驾，拈香礼佛。

　　这里有古老而又精密的轴承——转轮藏，现存最早的楷书碑刻《龙藏寺碑》，古代铜铸佛像中最高大的千手千眼观世音菩萨铜像，以及鲁迅眼中"东方美神"的观音泥塑。尤其值得一提的是被梁思成写入《中国建筑史》的摩尼殿，梁先生称其为"宋《营造法式》之典范，世界古建筑孤例"。寺中四时之景美而不同，春色澄灵，冬韵端严。游人缓步行至摩尼殿前，醒目的四面抱厦，曲线如波的高挑飞檐，恍惚置身宋画中，竟突然有些理解了梁思成初见此寺时说与妻子林徽因的那句赞叹——"使我们高兴到发狂"。

There is a famous temple hidden in Zhengding ancient city. This place used to be a royal garden, and a temple called Longcang was built in the garden during the reign of Wen Emperor of the Sui Dynasty (581-618). The temple was renamed Longxing in its expansion in later generations. Relics of Tang and Song dynasties, including architecture, sculptures, murals, and inscriptions, are abundant and so precious to be passed down generations. Therefore, Longxing Temple has been favored by the emperors in successive dynasties over hundreds of years to visit and worship the Buddha.

The Wheel Turner of Buddhist Canons — the ancient and sophisticated bearing, the earliest extant inscription in the regular script — Longcang Temple Stele, the largest bronze statue of Avalokitesvara Bodhisattva among ancient bronze Buddha statues, and the clay sculpture of Avalokitesvara which was praised by Lu Xun as the "Oriental Beauty Goddess" are kept in Longxing Temple. It is worth mentioning that the Manichean Hall was included in Liang Sicheng's *A History of Chinese Architecture*. Mr. Liang believed it as the "typical model of *Methods of Construction* created in the Song Dynasty, and the solitary example in ancient architecture in the world". Different beautiful scenes can be found in different seasons, such as clear spring and solemn winter. Walking slowly to the front of Manichean Hall, the travelers would feel like walking in a picture scroll in the Song Dynasty with eye-catching surrounding buildings and tall cornices with curves like waves and suddenly understand the admiration Liang Sicheng said to his wife Lin Huiyin when he first saw this temple, "… it drove us crazy with joy".

柏林禅寺
Bailin Temple

柏林禅寺位于河北赵县,千古名桥——赵州桥与其遥遥相望。这座古刹虽几经兴衰,却法脉绵延,高僧辈出。传说玄奘法师在西行印度取经之前,也曾在柏林禅寺研习经文。但真正让柏林禅寺名垂千古的,是唐代从谂禅师将茶文化引入禅宗,从此茶不再单纯是止渴之物,而是与禅宗结合,成为将人引向内省、修行之物,品茶变为一种精神享受。"禅茶一味"的观念至此从柏林禅寺传至全国,进而影响了东亚乃至整个世界。至今,世界茶道中人仍会定期聚会于柏林禅寺寻根溯源。

寺内这位禅茶大师的舍利塔巍峨矗立,精美壮观,方圆百里无出其右者。无论是丽景融晴之日,还是夕阳晚霞之间,古寺中的禅堂松韵、古塔斜阳都伴着阵阵茶香引导人们进入禅的世界。

Bailin Temple is located in Zhao County of Hebei Province, opposite to the famous ancient bridge — Zhaozhou Bridge in distance. Through numerous rises and falls, the ancient temple still sticks to promote Buddhist spirit and cultivate many eminent monks. Legend has it that Master Xuanzang also studied scriptures at the Bailin Temple before going on a pilgrimage for Buddhist scriptures to India. But what made the name of the Bailin Temple last forever was the introduction of tea culture by Master Congshen in the Tang Dynasty to Chan Buddhism. From then on, tea is no longer simply a thing for quenching thirst but is combined with Chan Buddhism, and it has become a thing that draws people to introspection and practice. Tasting tea becomes

a kind of spiritual enjoyment. The concept of "Combination of Tea and Zen" has spread from Bailin Temple to the whole country, and then to East Asia and the whole world. Even today, people worshiping teaism in the world still gather regularly at the Bailin Temple to trace the origin.

The Stupa of Master Congshen is the most majestic, exquisite, and magnificent building in the surrounding hundreds of miles. Whether it is in the beautiful daytime, or at sunset, the meditation rooms, pines, and towers in this ancient temple, as well as the setting sun all lead people in the world of Zen with the fragrance of tea.

保国寺
Baoguo Temple

保国寺坐落于宁波灵山之中，虽是千年古寺，却没有香火鼎盛，也没有多少传奇故事，更没有名人雅士的遗迹。直到20世纪中叶以后，一群研究古建筑的年轻人在荒山蔓草间发现了这座未经后人修饰过的千年古寺，人们才知有"保国寺"，才能窥得一丝大宋风雅的实貌。

保国寺如今已是一座中国古代建筑的博物馆，寺中保存了完好无损的宋代木构建筑与汉唐遗迹。于古寺的宋代大殿之中仰首而望，千载岁月流逝，却丝毫无损无梁殿精美绝伦的藻井、千变万化的斗拱，中华营造之美在古老大殿中回荡。中国古代建筑教科书《营造法式》曾被认为已无对应实物存世，可当保国寺大殿被发现后，这本难以解读的古书终于被世人读懂。千年古寺经历了门庭冷落和香火寂寥后，成为了一座独一无二的中国古代建筑博物馆，没有了青灯古佛、经书黄卷，却依然接受着人们对先人智慧与创造的膜拜。

Baoguo Temple is located in Ling Mountain near Ningbo City. Although it has a long history of over 1000 years, there are few visitors and little legends or relics of famous people. It is known to the world and shown its flavor of the Song Dynasty not until the mid-20th century when a group of young people studying ancient buildings discovered it in the wilderness.

Baoguo Temple is a museum of ancient Chinese architecture with the undamaged wooden architecture of the Song Dynasty and the relics of Han and Tang dynasties. Looking up in the ancient Wuliang Hall that was constructed in the Song Dynasty, the exquisite caisson ceiling and the ever-changing brackets of the Hall have not been damaged through thousands of years. The beauty of Chinese construction can be found everywhere in the ancient hall. It was once thought that there were no corresponding physical objects for the examples mentioned in the textbook of ancient Chinese architecture *Methods of Construction*, but when the main hall of Baoguo Temple was discovered, this ancient book that was once difficult to read was finally understood by the world. The thousand-year-old temple has become a unique ancient Chinese architectural museum after experiencing abandonment and loneliness. Without the Buddhist sculptures and scriptures, it still receives people's worship of the wisdom and creation of the ancestors.

04 佛光寺
Foguang Temple

中国的名山古寺似乎从来不缺乏引人入胜的传奇故事。五台山一向佛事极盛，而始建于北魏的佛光寺早在隋唐就已是五台山名刹，就连敦煌壁画中都有关于佛光寺华丽壮美的描绘。

然而20世纪初，国事日颓，佛光寺也荒废萧条，空门寂寞，几乎被世人遗忘。令古寺重回荣光的不是上天神佛的眷顾，而是建筑师的一双慧眼、一片热忱。梁思成、林徽因这对毕业于欧美名校的传奇伉俪，放弃了大都市的舒适繁华与名利，凭着他们对中国古代建筑的热忱走遍了中国的山野乡林，只为打破外国学者关于"中华大地已无唐代木构建筑之实物"的论断。当林徽因缓缓推开佛光寺东大殿的那扇沉重的门，人世间的光芒顷刻涌进古寺，照亮了千年香灰浮尘掩盖下的佛光寺，敦煌壁画中盛唐建筑辉煌灿烂的景象重回人间。或许那一瞬间的光，真的是"佛光"，它不但照亮了盛唐古寺，也照亮了中国建筑史，更照亮了中华民族的古老文明。

It seems like China's famous mountains and ancient temples never lack fascinating legends. Wutai Mountain has always been extremely prosperous in Buddhist affairs, and the Foguang Temple, which was built in the Northern Wei Dynasty (386-534), was already a famous temple on Wutai Mountain in the Sui and Tang dynasties. Even the Dunhuang frescoes contain the magnificent depiction of the Foguang Temple.

However, at the beginning of the 20th century, the country was weakening, and Foguang Temple was also deserted with few pilgrims, almost forgotten by the world. What brought the ancient temple back to glory was not the blessing of the gods or Buddhas, but the insight and enthusiasm of the architect. Liang Sicheng and Lin Huiyin, the legendary couple who graduated from famous European and American universities, gave up the comfort and prosperous life in the big city, as well as fame and fortune. They traveled across China's mountains and countryside with their passion for ancient Chinese architecture, just to break the conclusion of foreign scholars that "there is no real wood architecture of Tang Dynasty in China". When Lin Huiyin slowly opened the heavy door of the East Hall of the Foguang Temple, the light instantly flooded into the ancient Temple, illuminating the Foguang Temple under the incense dust of thousands of years, and the splendid scenes of architecture in the High Tang depicted in Dunhuang frescoes were coming back to life. Perhaps the light at that moment was the "Foguang" (Buddha light), which not only illuminates the ancient temple built in the High Tang but also illuminates the history of Chinese architecture and the ancient Chinese civilization.

05 华严寺
Huayan Temple

华严寺位于山西省大同市内。古寺始建于辽，曾经作为辽的太庙，因此按照契丹人敬日的习俗，该寺坐西朝东而建。明代重修后，华严寺便分成上、下寺两组建筑。今位于下寺的薄迦教藏殿、位于上寺的大雄宝殿，皆为辽金原物。大雄宝殿虽为金代重建，但辽韵犹存。大殿建于雄伟高台之上，气势宏大，尤其殿顶正脊上琉璃鸱尾高近五米，观者立于殿前，庄严肃穆之感油然而生。下寺薄迦教藏殿无论建筑还是雕塑皆为辽代原物。佛殿出檐深远、轮廓优美，殿中彩塑精美优雅，弥勒佛左外侧菩萨像被奉为中国古代雕塑的国宝。菩萨体态丰润，腰胯轻扭，身姿窈窕婀娜，双手于胸前合十，手指纤纤，露齿含笑。这笑容含蓄动人，当年郭沫若曾坐于此菩萨像前，静观一日仍觉不舍。近千年岁月浮尘和梵宫香灰，逐渐覆盖了遍身金箔的佛像，只有脸颊、关节等处依稀可见昔日灿烂明澄的华美金色。在殿内近乎幽暗的光线下，神秘与美在千年之中酝酿出这种令人迷醉的情景。

Huayan Temple is located in Datong City of Shanxi Province. The ancient temple was built in the Liao Dynasty (907-1125) and used to be the imperial ancestral temple. Therefore, according to the Khitan people's customs of worshiping the sun, it was built with the west facing the east. After the rebuilt in the Ming Dynasty, Huayan Temple was divided into two architectural sets: Upper Temple and Lower Temple. The Bojiajiaozang (Bhagavad Sutra Repository) at the lower Temple and the Mahavira Hall at the upper Temple are all built in Liao and Jin dynasties. Although the Mahavira Hall was rebuilt in the Jin Dynasty, it still shows some features of the Liao Dynasty. The main hall is built on a majestic high platform with a magnificent atmosphere, especially the glazed Chiwei on the roof ridge in the front is nearly 5 meters high. When the viewers stand in front of the hall, a sense of solemnity arises spontaneously. The architecture and sculptures of Bojiajiaozang at the lower Temple are passed down from the Liao Dynasty. The temple has far-reaching eaves and beautiful outlines. The colored sculptures in the temple are exquisite and elegant. The statue of Bodhisattva on the left side of Maitreya Buddha is regarded as a national treasure of ancient Chinese sculpture. This Bodhisattva has a plump body, lightly twisted waist and hips, and a bendy figure; palms are put together devoutly in front of the chest; he also has slender fingers and a toothy smile. This smile is subtle and moving. It is said that Guo Moruo once sat in front of this Bodhisattva, and still felt unwilling to leave after a day of contemplation. The Buddha statue with gold leaves is gradually covered with the floating dust and the incense ash in the past thousand years, only the faint traces at the cheeks and joints can make people think of its original gorgeous golden image. Under the dim light in the hall, this intoxicating scene was brewed in the mystery and beauty of one millennium.

06 智化寺
Zhihua Temple

北京东城的一片充满烟火气的胡同旧宅区内，隐藏着一座精美却内敛的古寺——智化寺。古寺虽身处市井，但逾几百载而未改旧貌，留下周身原汁原味的明代样貌。智化寺虽不宏大，但却晨钟暮鼓、佛殿阁堂齐全，梁架斗拱、藻井彩画俱在。各殿堂内经橱、佛像，乃至转轮藏尚存完好。古寺与众不同之处乃是留有梵音一脉，中国古代宫廷佛乐在这里经几百年而传承下来，至今仍有乐僧演奏佛乐。古寺之内遍植名花奇卉，晴和春暖之时最堪游此佳境。寺内院落重重，每院花却不同。初入古寺，满院丁香清幽；再入内院，则梨花雪白素雅；转入后院却玉兰海棠相竟而放，一派玉堂富贵之相。身处花海玉树间徜徉，抬头见古寺红墙黛瓦、梁画堆金、清风鸟语、花落无尘，耳畔佛音袅袅，心亦随佛乐梵音飞入九天。

In a hustle and bustle old Hutong in Dongcheng District of Beijing, there is an exquisite but restrained ancient temple — Zhihua Temple. Although the ancient temple is in the town, it has not changed its original appearance in the Ming Dynasty for hundreds of years. Although the Zhihua Temple is not large, it has a complete Buddhist architecture system of the morning bell, evening drum, halls, pavilions, beams, brackets, caisson ceiling, and colorful paintings. There are surpluses of scripture cabinets, Buddha statues, and even the wheel turner of Buddhist canons in the halls. The distinctive feature of this ancient temple is the Buddhist music. The Buddhist music played in ancient Chinese court has been passed down for hundreds of years and is intact here, and there are still monks playing Buddhist music today. The ancient temple is full of flowers and plants and is the best place to visit in sunny and warm spring. Different flowers are planted in different courtyards in the temple. On the first step into the ancient temple, the courtyard is full of lilacs; when entering the inner courtyard, the pear blossoms are white and elegant; and then entering the backyard, the magnolias and begonias are in full bloom for a prosperous scene. Wandering among the sea of flowers and trees, looking up to see the red walls, black tiles, beam paintings, golden decorations of the ancient temple, as well as feeling the breeze and falling flowers, hearing the birds whispering and the sound of Buddha chanting, our hearts also fly into the high sky with the Buddhist music and Sanskrit.

07 双林寺
Shuanglin Temple

　　双林寺位于山西省平遥古城外西南，与平遥古城作为一个整体，被列入世界文化遗产名录。该寺始建于五代，北宋时因释迦牟尼"双林入灭"之说，改称双林寺。如今，双林寺由十座风格各异的殿堂组成三进院落，寺中唐槐宋碑，元明彩塑、壁画虽已经被岁月磨去鲜艳的色彩，但其魅力丝毫不损，甚至有了一丝清水芙蓉的天然之感，更增添了许多古朴凝重的庄严。各殿中琳琅满目的彩塑，两千余尊，大的一丈有余，小的长不盈尺，这些虽然都是神仙佛像，但被赋予了凡间众生的特性，一颦一笑、一喜一嗔之间充满了世俗人物的喜怒哀乐之态。菩萨的安详自若，金刚力士的怒目圆睁，更像我们身边每一个有鲜明性格的普通人。古寺墙壁上那些雕塑群像灵活生动，意趣横生，将佛教传说演绎成市井人家的传奇故事。于是，这些曾经堆金沥粉的精美雕塑，在古寺香火寂寥之后，仍能以其不朽的艺术价值独立于世。

Shuanglin Temple is located in the southwest outside the ancient city of Pingyao in Shanxi. As a part of Pingyao, it is listed on the World Cultural Heritage List. The temple was built in the Five Dynasties period. In the Northern Song Dynasty, it was renamed Shuanglin Temple because of Sakyamuni's saying of "Passed away at Shuanglin". Today, Shuanglin Temple comprises of three courtyards consisting of ten halls with different styles. In the temple, the locust trees planted in the Tang Dynasty, steles of the Song Dynasty, the colored sculptures and murals of Yuan and Ming dynasties have been worn away their bright colors, but their charm has not been diminished. On the contrary, there is even a natural beauty that adds feelings of simplicity and solemnity to the temple. There are dazzling arrays of colored sculptures in the halls, the large ones are more than three meters high, and the small ones are not more than one foot. These two thousand sculptures of deities and Buddhas are endowed with the characteristics of mortal beings. Expressions of frowning, smiling, happiness and anger have reminded visitors of secular figures. The serene and calm Bodhisattvas and the glaring eyes of the Vajra warriors are more like every ordinary person around us with a distinct personality. The sculptures on the walls of the ancient temple are lively and interesting, and they interpret the Buddhist legends into the legendary folklore in the secular world. As a result, these exquisite sculptures that used to be covered with gold powder can still occupy a position in the world with their immortal artistic value even after the ancient temple was not prosperous as before.

08 佛宫寺
Buddha Palace Temple

佛宫寺位于山西省朔州市应县城西北，始建于五代，因寺内建有高耸入云的释迦塔（应县木塔）而闻名天下。这座宝塔不仅是存世的世界最高木塔，也是中国现存唯一一座木构建筑塔。千年来，经历了风霜雨雪的摧残、地震兵火的涂炭，砖石垒砌的古寺日益衰朽，而不用一钉一铁、仅用榫卯连接的古木塔却依然如故。明成祖、明武宗两位皇帝分别为木塔留下了"峻极神工""天下奇观"的匾额，而中国建筑学泰斗梁思成则叹其"绝对Overwhelming（势不可当）"。如今，我们驻足塔下，带着震撼敬佩之情，感受古代匠人精妙的技艺、高妙的智慧，以及它所代表的古老文明。

Buddha Palace Temple is located in the northwest of Ying County, Shuozhou City, Shanxi Province. It was built in the Five Dynasties period and is famous for the towering Sakyamuni Pagoda (Yingxian Wooden Pagoda) built in the temple. This pagoda is not only the existing tallest wooden tower in the world but also the only existing wooden tower in China. For one thousand years, the ancient temple built of bricks and stones has become increasingly decayed through natural disasters, earthquakes, and war fires, however, the ancient pagoda, which only uses mortise-tenon joints instead of nails and irons, remains the same. The two emperors of Chengzu and Wuzong of the Ming Dynasty respectively left plaques on the wooden pagoda of "Extreme Mastercraft" and "The Wonder of the World". And Liang Sicheng, a Chinese architecture Master, praised it as "Definite Overwhelming". Today, we stop and admire the tower, feeling the exquisite skills and wisdom of ancient craftsmen, and the ancient civilization it represents.

09 镇国寺
Zhenguo Temple

  镇国寺位于山西平遥古城外。春秋迭代,镇国寺屡有修葺,尽管没有什么名山大川和文人墨客的加持,但胜在古迹之悠久精绝。

  镇国寺中的万佛殿是中国现存最早的木构建筑之一,虽是五代建筑,却有大唐风韵。万佛殿单檐歇山,出檐深远,更显唐制庄重,且不用一钉,俱是榫卯相接,犹存大唐昔日营造之美。殿内十一尊塑像皆是五代遗珍,神像体态丰腴,姿态面貌安谧柔美,亦可见唐风于五代中的遗韵悠长。寺中尚有元代天王殿、金代铜钟、明代泥塑等历代珍品。千年间,镇国寺始终泰然自若,俗世纷乱似乎止步于古寺山门之前,院中古树虬曲苍劲,绿荫如盖,在岁月静好中悠然地从虔诚的香火绕殿变为了古迹遗珍。

Zhenguo Temple is located outside Pingyao Ancient City of Shanxi Province. Over the passing years, Zhenguo Temple had been repaired frequently. Although there is no blessing from famous natural spots or literati, it is good enough to be appreciated for its long and exquisite historical sites.

Wanfo Hall in Zhenguo Temple is one of the earliest existing wooden architecture in China. It was built in the Five Dynasties period but has some features of the Tang Dynasty. Wanfo Hall has a single-eave hipped-roof with long eaves, which shows the solemn style of Tang. And there is no nail but mortise-tenon joints to connect the structure, which is the typical construction style of the Tang Dynasty. The eleven statues in the hall are all treasures constructed in the Five Dynasties period. These statues are plump in the posture with peaceful and soft faces, which also represent the trace of Tang style in the architecture of the Five Dynasties period. There are also treasures, such as Hall of Heavenly Kings of the Yuan Dynasty, the bronze bell of the Jin Dynasty, and the clay sculpture of the Ming Dynasty that are protected in the temple. For one thousand years, Zhenguo Temple has always been poised, and the chaos of the secular world seems to stop at the gate of the ancient temple. Under the rough shady trees in the courtyard, this temple quietly turned itself from a temple for pious pilgrims to a place for retaining the heritage of ancient relics.

 法海寺
Fahai Temple

法海寺位于北京市石景山区的翠微山南麓，山谷幽静，峰峦绵亘，松林葱郁，景色宜人。周围的苍松巨柏给这座建于明朝中期的古老寺庙增添了勃勃生机。

法海寺素以大雄宝殿内的十幅保留完好的明代壁画著称于世。法海寺壁画与敦煌壁画、永乐宫壁画相比各有千秋，是元明清以来现存少有的由宫廷画师绘制的精美壁画。观此壁画，恍如佛国天宫重现尘寰。壁画以工笔重彩绘成，色彩叠晕烘染，运笔技法精湛，沥粉堆金更显饱满辉煌，大处气势磅礴，小处精致入微，突显了法缘殊胜的佛界庄严，犹如圆融无碍的华藏世界，宛然万象，耀人心田。

Fahai Temple is located in the southern foothills of Cuiwei Mountain in Shijingshan District of Beijing, where there is a quiet valley, endless peaks and ridges, lush pine forest, and pleasant scenery. The surrounding green pines and giant cypresses add vitality to this ancient temple built in the middle of the Ming Dynasty.

Fahai Temple is well known for its ten well-preserved Ming Dynasty murals in its Mahavira Hall. Compared with Dunhuang frescoes and murals in Yongle Palace, murals in Fahai Temple have their features because they are the existing rare exquisite murals painted by court painters since the Yuan, Ming, and Qing dynasties. The murals seem to reproduce the Buddha's Heavenly Palace to the world. The murals are painted with meticulous brushwork, overlapping colors, and exquisite techniques. Lifen-Duijin technique (Plaster-Squeezing and Gilding) shows the fullness and splendor of the picture with the majestic atmosphere and delicate and subtle details. These murals have depicted a majestic Buddha realm with exceptional dharma, just like the harmonious and unobstructed Avatamsaka World. Everything in the murals is just like everything in people's hearts.

独乐寺
Dule Temple

独乐寺位于天津市蓟州区，相传始建于唐代。辽代，独乐寺重建，因此现存主要建筑观音阁和山门皆为辽代遗珍。观音阁外形檐出深远、稳重舒展，是中国最古老的楼阁建筑。建筑外观为两层，但内部包含一个暗层，内部的六边形筒状空间，用于安放一尊高约十六米的观音像。这尊观音菩萨宝相庄严，眉目低垂，身躯粗壮奇伟，是现存为数不多的男像观音造型。佛像全身比例协调，胸饰璎珞，细巧华美，整体造型富丽华贵，是中国古代雕塑的国宝级珍品。佛像头顶十个小头像分作四层环列四周，因此这座佛像也被称为"十一面观音"。若站于楼阁高处观赏，无论从哪个角度看，皆有一面可与观者对望，十分精妙。

古寺尚存元代壁画，这些壁画曾在几百年前被白灰覆盖，20世纪70年代整修时才复现人间。古寺处兵家必争的渔阳重镇，历经千年几番兵燹而不毁，仍矗立于燕赵大地，成为世人瞻仰唐风辽韵的悠悠大观。

Dule Temple is located in Jizhou District of Tianjin City. Words have it that this temple was built in the Tang Dynasty. In the Liao Dynasty, Dule Temple was rebuilt, so the existing main buildings, Avalokitesvara Pavilion and the Gate are both treasures of the Liao Dynasty. The Avalokitesvara Pavilion is the oldest pavilion building in China with far-reaching eaves. The building is in two-story, but the interior contains a dark layer, and the internal hexagonal cylindrical space is used to house an Avalokitesvara statue about 16 meters high. This Avalokitesvara statue has a solemn appearance, drooping eyes and eyebrows, and a sturdy majestic body. It is one of the few existing statues of Avalokitesvara in male form. This statue has a coordinated proportion, wears delicate and beautiful jewelry of precious stones on the chest, and is in magnificent and luxurious shape. It is a national treasure of ancient Chinese sculpture. Ten small heads on the top of the statue are arranged in four layers, so it is also called "Eleven-faced Avalokitesvara". If you stand on the higher place of the pavilion, you can look into the eye of the statue from any angle, that's the subtlety lies in.

There are also some murals from the Yuan Dynasty in this ancient temple. These murals were covered with white ash hundreds of years ago and only reappeared when they were renovated in the 1970s. The ancient temple is located in Yuyang town which was an important battleground for military strategists. After thousands of years of wars, the temple still stands on the land of ancient Yan and Zhao Kingdoms and has become an ideal temple to appreciate the charm of the Tang and Liao dynasties.

12 奉国寺
Fengguo Temple

　　奉国寺位于辽宁省锦州市义县，县城虽小，但是当你真正来到这里的时候，你会惊讶地发现，这座神秘的古寺曾见证了两个朝代的荣耀。

　　奉国寺始建于辽，保存着中国最大的辽代殿堂建筑，也是中国现存古建筑中最大的单层木结构建筑。寺内主体建筑大雄殿及寺院整体，上承唐代遗风，下启辽金等寺院布局，是辽金寺院中最具典型性的例证。其中，大雄殿代表了辽代佛教建筑的最高成就，殿内尚存世所罕见的古老而又庞大的彩色泥塑佛像群。这七尊辽代塑像，经历岁月流逝，几番人间迭废，佛像上鲜艳的堆金沥粉早已斑驳，但当人们静立于佛像之下，却更觉天地之悠悠。

　　Fengguo Temple is located in Yixian County, Jinzhou City, Liaoning Province. The county is small, but when you come here, you will be surprised to find that this mysterious ancient temple has witnessed the glory of two dynasties.

　　Fengguo Temple was built in the Liao Dynasty and preserves the largest palace building of the Liao Dynasty in China which is also the largest existing single-story wooden structure in ancient Chinese architecture. The main building of the temple, the Mahavira Hall, as well as the whole temple is the most typical example of the temple layout in the Liao and Jin dynasties which inherited the Tang style and enlightened its followers. Among them, the Mahavira Hall represents the highest achievement of Buddhist architecture in the Liao Dynasty and preserves the rare ancient and huge group of colored clay Buddha statues in the world. The seven statues of the Liao Dynasty have gone through times and witnessed rises and falls in the world. The bright gold powder on the Buddha statues has long been mottled, but when people stand before the Buddha statues, they feel more relaxed and relieved.

开元寺
Kaiyuan Temple

　　开元寺位于广东省潮州市，始建于唐代开元盛世，因此后世俗称此寺为"开元寺"并沿用至今。千载间，古寺香火鼎盛，信众捐资维修，雕梁画栋，池台竹树，必极工巧。所以，开元寺不仅保留了盛唐初建时的布局，还遗存了宋、元、明、清各个朝代的精美建筑。

　　古寺所处的粤东潮汕地区，海岸线漫长曲折，是"海上丝绸之路"的重要港口，精美的中国瓷器就是从这里被运往全世界的。因此，建筑屋顶上的嵌瓷艺术成为本地传统建筑物的一大特色。开元寺中，无论是天王殿顶的双龙戏珠，还是屋脊两端的龙吐楚尾花，都玲珑曲折、动态盎然。大雄宝殿上则是姿态优美的双凤朝牡丹和镇火的宝葫芦，各殿屋檐之上还有各类佛教人物，都极致精巧、活灵活现。东方古瓷的光泽和色彩与中国古典建筑的庄重严肃在这里奇妙地融合出一种流光溢彩的美感。

Kaiyuan Temple is located in the Chaozhou City of Guangdong Province. It was built in the prosperous period of Kaiyuan in the Tang Dynasty. Therefore, it was later commonly called "Kaiyuan Temple" and the name is passed on up to now. For thousands of years, the ancient temple has received a lot of incense from pilgrims and maintenance funds donated by the believers. With the money, the construction in the temple, such as the carved beams and painted buildings, pools, and bamboo trees, are all in extremely skilled craftsmanship. Therefore, Kaiyuan Temple not only retains the layout of Tang style when it is first built, but also preserves the exquisite buildings of the Song, Yuan, Ming, and Qing dynasties.

The Chaozhou-Shantou region in eastern Guangdong where the ancient temple is located has a long and winding coastline and is an important port on the "Maritime Silk Road", from which exquisite Chinese porcelain was shipped to the world. Therefore, the art of inlaying porcelain on the roof of the building has become a major feature of the local traditional buildings. In Kaiyuan Temple, whether it is the Two Dragons Frolicking with a Pearl on the top of Hall of Heavenly Kings or the Dragon Spitting the Chuwei Flower at both ends of the ridge, all are exquisitely twisted and dynamic. The graceful Two Phoenix Facing the Peony and the Fire-suppressing Gourd in the Mahavira Hall and other various Buddhist figures on the eaves of other halls are all extremely delicate and vivid. The luster and color of oriental ancient porcelain and the solemnity of Chinese classical architecture wonderfully blend here with a sense of beauty.

光孝寺
Guangxiao Temple

光孝寺历史悠久，最早可追溯到公元前2世纪，当时是南越王赵建德的故宅。三国时期成了吴国虞翻的苑囿，虞翻去世后，虞苑被改成寺庙。后几经改名，最终于南宋定名为光孝寺。因此，在漫漫历史长河中，光孝寺保留下来了众多文物史迹，如始建于东晋的大雄宝殿，南朝的洗钵泉，唐朝时期为纪念六祖惠能而建的瘗发塔，宋明时期的卧佛殿，以及历代碑刻、佛像等。据传，瘗发塔大殿后还有一株虞翻种植的千年诃子树，可谓千古遗珍。

光孝寺气势雄伟，尤以具有唐宋建筑艺术风格的大雄宝殿为最。宝殿神龛上供奉的是"一佛两菩萨"，即"华严三圣"：中间为释迦牟尼如来佛，左边是大智菩萨文殊师利，右边是大行菩萨普贤。而在大佛腹中发现的唐代文物——木雕罗汉像，更是难得的中国木雕技艺的精品。

走进古寺，靠近那棵诃子树，尤可遥想千年前虞翻在种了许多诃子树的"诃林"里讲学的情境。

The Guangxiao Temple has a long history that can be dated back to the 2nd century BC when it was the home of Zhao Jiande, king of the Southern Yue Kingdom. During the Three Kingdoms period, it became the garden of Yu Fan in Wu State. After his death, Yu's Garden was converted into a temple. This ancient temple was renamed several times and was finally named Guangxiao Temple in the Southern Song Dynasty. Therefore, Guangxiao Temple has preserved many cultural and historical relics in the long history of China, such as the Mahavira Hall that was built in the Eastern Jin Dynasty, the Earthen bowl Spring in the Southern dynasties, the Hair Burying Tower in the Tang Dynasty to commemorate the Sixth Patriarch of the Chinese Chan Buddhism, Master Huineng, and the Mahaparinirvana Hall in the Song and Ming dynasties, as well as inscriptions and Buddha statues of the successive dynasties. According to legend, there is a thousand-year-old myrobalan tree planted by Yu Fan behind the main hall of Hair Burying Tower, which is a real treasure for over one thousand years.

The majesty of Guangxiao Temple is especially represented by the Mahavira Hall, which has the architectural style of Tang and Song dynasties. The hall enshrines "one Buddha and two Bodhisattva", that is, the "Three Sages of Huayan": in the middle is Shakyamuni Tathagata, to the left is Manjusri Bodhisattva, and to the right is Samantabhadra. And the cultural relic of the Tang Dynasty found in the belly of the Big Buddha — a wood carving Arhat statue is of rare Chinese woodcarving craftsmanship.

Walking into the ancient temple and approaching the myrobalan tree, the situation of Yu Fan giving lectures in Yu's Garden where many myrobalan trees were planted thousands of years ago still can be imagined.

15 岩山寺
Yanshan Temple

　　岩山寺位于陕西省繁峙县，这里是佛教名山五台山的山脚处。一千多年前，这里也是重要的战场，如今静谧无言的名山古树早已看尽了人间的厮杀与悲情。后人在此建筑了寺庙，希望通过佛教慈悲的力量让战死的将士安息。

　　古寺虽然在千年间迭经兴废，却奇迹般地保留了许多极其罕见的金代遗存——采用减柱法的文殊殿建筑，充满世俗意趣的观音雕像，以及"画在墙壁上的《清明上河图》"金代壁画。壁画的创作者是当时著名的宫廷画家，因此在他的画笔下不但有宝相庄严的诸神和美丽浪漫的天堂，同时也有细节真实的当时的宫廷建筑。现实世界中这些美丽的皇宫早已消失，只有站在这面壁画前，我们才得以窥得那个时代帝王皇宫华丽而又神秘的面貌。若非朱漆斑驳的窗牖之间那金色细碎的光影闪动，我们竟丝毫不觉自己的神思早已飞跃千年，遁入那一壁恢宏的仙山楼阁之中。

　　Yanshan Temple is located in Fanzhi County of Shaanxi Province, at the foot of the famous Buddhist Mountain — Wutai Mountain. More than a thousand years ago, Wutai Mountain was an important battlefield in ancient China. Today, the quiet and silent mountains and trees have experienced too much fighting and sadness in the world. Later generations built the temple here, hoping that through the power of compassion in Buddhism, the soldiers who died here could rest in peace.

　　Although the ancient temple has gone through ups and downs over thousands of years, it has miraculously preserved many extremely rare relics in the Jin Dynasty — the Manjusri Palace built with the column-reducing method, the Avalokitesvara statue full of secular taste, and the murals of the Jin Dynasty that were praised as the "*Riverside Scene at Qingming Festival* on the wall". The creator of the murals was a well-known court painter then, so he painted not only the majestic deities and the beautiful and romantic paradise but also the details of the real court architecture at that time. These beautiful palaces in the real world have long disappeared. Only these murals can enable us to get a glimpse of the gorgeous and mysterious imperial palaces of that era. If it hadn't been for the golden light and shadow between the vermillion-lacquered and mottled window sheets, we would not have realized that our minds had already leaped thousands of years, and escaped into that magnificent fairy mountain pavilion.

显通寺
Xiantong Temple

　　显通寺位于山西五台山台怀镇北侧。相传，两位天竺高僧迦叶摩腾、竺法兰在白马寺建成以后，从洛阳来到五台山，于东汉明帝永平年间，建起了"中国第二古寺"——显通寺。

　　这座古老的寺庙坐北朝南，中轴线上有观音殿、文殊殿、大雄宝殿、无量殿、千钵殿、铜殿和藏经殿七座殿宇。其中铜殿，据记载是明万历皇帝为感念母恩而铸造的，用铜五万公斤，是中国国内保存最好的铜殿之一。千钵殿中的文殊铜象，上顶五个头，胸前六只手，背后还有一千只手，且每只手上都有一个金钵，每个钵内都有一尊释迦牟尼佛，故又被称为千臂千钵千释迦文殊像。原用于收藏经书的藏经殿，现存各类文物——济公和尚瓷像，苏武牧羊花瓶，木雕善财童子和观音，水晶塔、银塔和各色景泰蓝供件等手工艺品，以及元初赵子昂夫妇画的马和观音，明沈周绘的关云长，由六十万字《华严经》组成的字塔等书画作品。可谓所到之处、所见之物皆是珍贵文物。徜徉其间，仿佛在聆听它们诉说古老且传奇的历史故事。

Xiantong Temple is located on the north side of Taihuai Town near Wutai Mountain of Shanxi Province. The legend goes that after the completion of the White Horse Temple, two eminent monks Kāśyapa Matanga and Zhu Falan came from Luoyang to Wutai Mountain and built the "Second Ancient Temple in China" — Xiantong Temple during the Yongping period under the reign of Emperor Ming of the Eastern Han Dynasty.

　　This ancient temple faces south and there are seven halls on its central axis, namely the Avalokitesvara Hall, the Manjusri Hall, the Mahavira Hall, the Wuliang Hall, the Qianbo Hall, the Copper Hall, and the Tripitaka Sutra Hall. According to records, the Copper Hall was built by the Emperor Wanli of the Ming Dynasty to express his gratitude to his mother. It was made of 50,000 kilograms of copper and is one of the best-preserved copper halls in China. The bronze statue of Manjusri in the Qianbo Hall has five heads, six hands in front, and a thousand hands on the back. Each hand has a golden bowl, and each bowl contains a statue of Shakyamuni. So it is also known as the thousand-arm, thousand-bowl, and thousand-Sakyamuni Manjusri Statue. The Tripitaka Sutra Hall was originally used for the preservation of scriptures, and now it is used for the preservation of various cultural relics — the porcelain statue of the Mad Monk, the vase of the Shepherd Suwu, the woodcarving Sudhana and Avalokitesvara, the crystal tower, the silver tower, and various cloisonne offerings and other handicrafts, as well as the paintings of horse and Avalokitesvara, painted by Zhao Zi'ang and his wife in the early Yuan Dynasty, the figure painting of Guan Yu by Shen Zhou in the Ming Dynasty, the calligraphy tower composed of the 600,000-character *Avatamsaka Sutra*, and other calligraphy and painting works. The place you visit and the objects you see are all precious cultural relics. Please walk around the temple to enjoy the ancient and legendary historical stories.

崇福寺
Chongfu Temple

唐代麟德二年（665），大将军尉迟敬德奉旨建造崇福寺。这是位于山西省朔州市一处规模宏大、古朴庄严的古寺庙。

崇福寺为五进院落，有天王殿、千佛阁、文殊堂、地藏殿、三宝殿、弥陀殿、观音殿等十座殿宇。其主殿——弥陀殿，是寺内最大的殿堂，供奉着保存完整、塑法古朴精美的金代雕像"西方三圣"——阿弥陀佛（中）、观音菩萨（左）、大势至菩萨（右）。位于弥陀殿之后的观音殿，有明代塑像三尊——观音菩萨（中）、文殊菩萨（左）、普贤菩萨（右）。崇福寺内的建筑、塑像、壁画、琉璃脊饰、雕花门窗、木雕楼阁形佛龛均保存完好，它是一座历史文化价值较高的古建艺术殿堂，虽历经风雨寒暑，仍焕发光彩。

In the second year of the Linde period of the Tang Dynasty, General Yuchi Jingde was ordered to build the Chongfu Temple. This is a magnificent, simple, and solemn ancient temple located in the Shuozhou City of Shanxi Province.

Chongfu Temple is a five-courtyard complex with ten temple halls including Hall of Heavenly Kings, Thousand Buddha Pavilion, Manjusri Hall, Ksitigarbharaja Hall, Triratna Hall, Amitabha Hall, and Avalokitesvara Hall. Its main hall, Amitabha Hall, is the largest in the temple. It enshrines the well-preserved, simple and exquisite statues of "Three Sages of the West" — Amitabha (middle), Avalokitesvara (left), and Mahasthamaprapta (right), which were made in the Jin Dynasty. Avalokitesvara Hall behind Amitabha Hall preserves Ming statues of Avalokitesvara (middle), Manjushri (left) and Samantabhadra (right). The buildings, statues, murals, glazed ridge decorations, carved doors and windows, and wood-carved pavilion-shaped Buddhist altars in Chongfu Temple are well-preserved. It is an ancient art palace with high historical and cultural value.

安国寺
Anguo Temple

安国寺始建于唐贞观年间，位于山西省吕梁市的乌崖山麓。古寺依山而建，石头围墙高低起伏，四周松柏绿林葱郁，远观俨然一处若隐若现的古寨堡。

安国寺在金、元、明历代皆有修葺。其中，大雄宝殿是单檐悬山式木结构建筑，虽为元代建筑，却有唐代遗风。而寺后在天然形成的庞大石崖下修筑的莱公别墅，地势险要，景色奇特，构筑精巧，可谓融人工与天工、人文精神与自然环境于一体。若遇雨天，于千仞绝壁下，则可观悬崖飞瀑，水帘垂挂，甚为壮观。

乌崖山山势沿南坡自然围拢成两臂环抱状，其间翠柏林立，与片石山岩纵横交错，云雾缭绕迷蒙，山路百转千回，与安国寺院参差错落的青瓦屋宇、峭壁上光影生动的孔孔石窟，相映生辉，恰似天公的精心安排，体现了中国传统建筑高超的山水美学意境——"融"。

Anguo Temple was built during the Zhenguan period of the Tang Dynasty and is located at the foot of Wuya Mountain in Lvliang, Shanxi Province. The ancient temple was built on the hillside, with undulating stone walls, surrounded by lush green pine and cypress forests, and looks like a looming old castle from a distance.

Anguo Temple was repaired in the Jin, Yuan, and Ming dynasties. Among them, the Mahavira Hall is a single-eave overhanging-roof wooden structure. Although it is built in the Yuan Dynasty, it has some features of the Tang Dynasty. The Laigong Villa built under the natural huge stone cliffs behind the temple has dangerous terrain, peculiar scenery, and exquisite construction. It can be seen as a combination of artificial and natural engineering, humanistic spirit, and natural environment. Standing under the high cliffs on rainy days, people can enjoy the spectacular scene of waterfalls running down the cliffs to form a water curtain.

The Wuya Mountain is naturally surrounded by two ridges along the south slope, lush cypresses are crisscrossing with the mountain rocks, and the mountain roads are shrouded with clouds and mists. The natural beauty is reflected with the blue-tiled houses, the numerous caves on the cliffs in Anguo Temple, which looks like heaven's meticulous arrangement and embodies the superb landscape aesthetic conception of traditional Chinese architecture — "Harmony".

19 灵山寺
Lingshan Temple

　　灵山寺据传始建于唐初，位于河南省洛阳市凤凰山北麓，亦名"凤凰寺"。灵山寺依山就势，南高北低，苍老挺拔的千年银杏，萦绕寺前的山溪，风景幽美。

　　灵山寺现存建筑有山门阁、中佛殿、天王殿、大雄宝殿、藏经楼、东西祖师楼等，其中大悲阁、大雄宝殿梁柱仍为金代建筑。大雄宝殿内有河南省现存最早的泥塑作品——明朝佛像三尊，即"三世佛"。始建于清代的山门，是灵山寺的北大门，下部为一砖筑平台，上建单檐歇山顶式阁楼一座，风格独特。此外，十七座明清两代高僧的砖石墓塔，是中国现存的八处塔群之一。现今，灵山寺的建筑布局大体为金代创建，经明清两代整修后保留下来，具有一定的历史和艺术研究价值。

According to legend, Lingshan Temple was built in the early Tang Dynasty and is located at the northern foot of the Phoenix Mountain in Luoyang City, Henan Province, also known as the "Phoenix Temple". Lingshan Temple is situated on the hillside, high in the south and low in the north. It has beautiful scenery with upright ginkgoes over one thousand years in the temple and a mountain stream lingering in front of the temple.

The existing buildings of Lingshan Temple include the Gate Pavilion, the Central Buddha Hall, Hall of Heavenly Kings, the Mahavira Hall, the Tripitaka Sutra Building, and the East and West Zushi Buildings, etc. Among them, the Great Compassion Pavilion and the beams and columns of the Mahavira Hall are relics of the Jin Dynasty. In the Mahavira Hall, there are the three Buddha statues, "Buddhas of Three Periods", which are the earliest surviving clay sculptures in Henan Province. The mountain gate, built in the Qing Dynasty, is the north gate of Lingshan Temple. The lower part is a brick platform, on top of which there is a pavilion of single-eave hipped-roof in unique style. In addition, the 17 masonry tomb towers of eminent monks in the Ming and Qing dynasties are one of the eight existing tower complexes in China. The architectural layout of Lingshan Temple today was generally created in the Jin Dynasty, and it has been preserved after renovation in the Ming and Qing dynasties. It has certain historical and artistic value.

20 铁佛寺
Iron Buddha Temple

　　与"沧州狮子景州塔"相媲美的"东光县的铁菩萨",指的就是铁佛寺中的铁铸释迦牟尼佛像。它位于铁佛寺大雄宝殿之中,高八米多,重四万八千千克,是我国最大的座式铸铁佛像。

　　铁佛寺位于河北省沧州市,始建于北宋开宝五年（972）。其主要建筑包括山门、天王殿和大雄宝殿。其中,大雄宝殿是寺内的主体建筑,为单檐歇山式。殿前有抱厦,檐下有由著名书法家溥杰所书的"大雄宝殿"金字匾额。四字流畅活泼,为庄严的宝殿增添了灵动与活力。现今的铁佛寺以"红"显著——红色的山门、红色的围墙、红色的圆柱、红色的窗棂,蔚为壮观,恰似一颗红宝石。

The "Iron Bodhisattva of Dongguang County" comparable to "Lion Statue in Cangzhou and Jingzhou Tower" refers to the iron-cast Sakyamuni Statue in Iron Buddha Temple. It is set in the Mahavira Hall of Iron Buddha Temple. It is more than eight meters high and weighs 48,000 kilograms, and is the largest seated iron-cast Buddha statue in China.

Iron Buddha Temple is located in Cangzhou City, Hebei Province. It was built in the fifth year of Kaibao period in the Northern Song Dynasty. Its main buildings include the mountain gate, Hall of Heavenly Kings, and the Mahavira Hall. The Mahavira Hall is the major building of the temple with a single-eave hipped-roof. Under the roof of the affiliated room in front of the hall, there is a plaque with gold characters "the Mahavira Hall" written by the famous calligrapher Pu Jie. The four characters are in a fluent and lively style, adding a lot of liveliness and vitality to the solemn temple. Today's Iron Buddha Temple is notable for the color "red" — the red gate, the red wall, the red column, and the red window mullions. It is so magnificent that it looks like a ruby.

21 毗卢寺
Pilu Temple

以精美的古代壁画而闻名的毗卢寺，位于河北省石家庄市，始建于唐天宝年间（742—756），因毗卢殿中央佛台上供奉的本尊主佛毗卢遮那而得名。

该寺的毗卢殿和释迦殿内均绘有壁画，是我国目前保存较为完好的明代壁画之一。毗卢寺的壁画内容丰富，上下分三排，绘有天堂、地狱、人间，有罗汉、菩萨等各种人物五百多位，形象生动逼真。壁画以石绿、朱红为色彩基调，在强烈的对比色中取得和谐，沥粉贴金更给壁画增添了光彩。整个壁画线条娴熟，技艺精湛，具有较高的艺术价值，对研究古代美术史和传统绘画艺术具有重要的意义，是我国古代壁画的遗宝。几百个春夏秋冬过去，毗卢寺的壁画虽历经沧桑，但仍光彩夺目。

Pilu Temple, known for its exquisite ancient murals, is located in Shijiazhuang City, Hebei Province. It was built during the Tianbao period of the Tang Dynasty (742-756) and named after the main Buddha Vairocana (Pilu in Chinese) enshrined on the central altar of the Pilu Hall.

Murals are painted in Pilu Hall and Shijia Hall, which are some of the most well-preserved murals in the Ming Dynasty in China. The murals of Pilu Temple are rich in content, divided into three rows up and down, depicting heaven, hell, and the world. There are more than 500 figures of Confucianism, Buddhism, and Taoism, including Arhat, Bodhisattva, and loyal ministers. The murals use stone green and vermilion as the color base to achieve harmony in the strong contrasting colors. In addition, Lifen-Duijin technique (Plaster-Squeezing and Gilding) also adds luster to the murals. The entire mural paintings have high-skilled lines and craftsmanship and are of high artistic value. They are of great significance to the study of ancient art history and traditional painting art. They are the legacy of ancient Chinese murals. The murals of Pilu Temple have gone through hundreds of years of vicissitudes but maintain the dazzling charm.

22 灵岩寺
Lingyan Temple

灵岩寺始建于金代，位于河北省蔚县城内鼓楼西街。据传，是引发中国历史重大事件——"土木堡之变"的关键人物、明代司礼监太监王振奏请明英宗敕建此寺。重建后的灵岩寺具有明代官式建筑的独特风格。大雄宝殿的庑殿顶、藻井天花均华丽精致、用材考究，历数百载仍完好如初。大殿入口处六角菱花镂空落地隔扇将阳光细细筛过，温柔地洒入大殿，仰首红白二色折枝牡丹伴着盘龙、飞鹤盘旋于殿顶中央。极富感染力的艺术效果及浓郁厚重的宗教氛围，引人不知不觉间心生敬畏。踏出此殿，不远处的天王殿出檐深远，端庄稳重，充满了浓浓的金元遗韵。

Lingyan Temple was first built in the Jin Dynasty and is located on West Gulou Street in Yuxian County. It is said that Wang Zhen, a eunuch from Silijian in the Ming Dynasty, pleaded with Emperor Ying to build this temple. Wang Zhen was a key person who triggered the "Revolution of Tumu Fort", which was a major event in China's history. The reconstructed Lingyan Temple has the unique style of official architecture of the Ming Dynasty. The hip roof and carvings on the caisson ceiling of the Mahavira Hall are gorgeous and exquisite in sophisticated materials, and they are still intact after hundreds of years. At the entrance to the main hall, the hexagonal diamond-flower hollow floor-standing partitions sift the sunlight through and gently scatter it into the main hall. The red and white folded branch peony is accompanied by a dragon and a flying crane hovering in the center of the top of the hall. The contagious artistic effect and the strong religious atmosphere solemnized people unknowingly. Stepping out of this hall, the far-reaching-eave Hall of Heavenly Kings not far away looks dignified and steady, full of rich flavors of Jin and Yuan dynasties.

23 炳灵寺
Bingling Temple

甘肃省永靖县有一座古寺常年隐没在黄河深处。在这高峡之中、丹崖之下，今日造访的游人已经很难想象这里曾是千年前丝绸之路的要冲。那时候，常有串串清脆的驼铃声在空中回荡。这里是中原通向河西走廊、青藏高原，甚至是更遥远的西域诸国的交汇点，西北的多条重要河流也在此汇入黄河。于是宗教、艺术与文化便也在此处融合，人们利用悬崖两侧红砂岩上的天然凹凸修建了大量的佛教石窟。彼时，达官显贵，商贾信众皆来此礼佛。

"炳灵"是一句藏语，大意是"十万佛"，而古寺中几百处石窟洞，近千平方米的壁画，还有那无数的佛教雕塑大致也担得起寺名中的这个"十万佛"。但随着古代丝绸之路的驼铃声渐渐寂静，炳灵寺也失去了往昔盛况，震撼人心的石窟造像也在一片静谧中安然幽思，静静地等待着游人在佛陀的微笑中感受丝绸之路的山河旧梦。

There is an ancient temple hidden in the depths of the Yellow River all year round in Yongjing County, Gansu Province. In the middle of this high gorge and under the red cliffs, it is hard for visitors today to imagine that this place once was the road hub of the "Silk Road" thousands of years ago. At that time, there were often strings of crisp camel bells echoing in the air. It is the intersection of the Central Plains to the Hexi Corridor, the Qinghai-Xizang Plateau, and even more distant countries in the Western Regions. Many important rivers in the northwest also flow into the Yellow River here. As a result, religion, art, and culture also merged here, and finally, people built a large number of Buddhist caves using the natural bumps on the red sandstone on both sides of the cliffs in the years that followed. At that time, dignitaries and nobles, merchants and believers all came here to pay homage to the Buddha.

"Bingling" is originated from a Zang word with the meaning of "a hundred thousand Buddhas". The hundreds of caves in the ancient temple, nearly a thousand square meters of murals, and countless Buddhist sculptures can quite match the name of "a hundred thousand Buddhas". But as the camel bell of the ancient Silk Road gradually quieted, Bingling Temple also lost its past grandeur, and the thrilling grotto statues were meditating in silence, waiting for visitors to feel the old dream of mountains and rivers on the Silk Road in the Buddha's smile.

24 兴国寺
Xingguo Temple

兴国寺坐落在甘肃省天水秦安县，始建于元代。古时，天水是丝绸之路上的必经之地，名闻遐迩的玉门关见证了金戈铁马间的王朝交替，也看尽了古刹兴国寺的几番兴废。

现存的古寺建筑群仍基本完好，尤其是般若殿，虽经历代多次重修，但梁架结构，斗拱风格，基本上保持了元代建筑的特征。大殿正脊雕刻精美，游龙与西蕃莲灵动写实。殿顶的鸱吻怒目卷尾，似乎正在张口吞食屋脊。屋脊两侧按等距排列着绿色琉璃走兽。大殿门前一块醒目的"般若"匾额，仅白底黑字，不施粉彩，毫无凡俗之态，于朴拙之中尽显气度。丝路的驼铃声声悠扬，古寺在沧桑的岁月中守护着"般若"的智慧，也悄然融入了塞外大漠孤烟与长河落日的雄奇气象。

Xingguo Temple is located in Qin'an County of Tianshui in Gansu Province and was built in the Yuan Dynasty. In ancient times, Tianshui was a gateway on the Silk Road. The well-known Yumen Pass witnessed the change of dynasties in wars and the rises and falls of the ancient Xingguo Temple.

The existing ancient temple building complex is still basically intact, especially the Prajna Hall. Although it has been rebuilt many times in history, the beam structure and bracket-style retain the architectural characteristics of the Yuan Dynasty. The ridge of the main hall is exquisitely carved, and the dragon and passion lotus are vivid. The glaring Chiwen on the top of the temple curling its tail in anger is swallowing the roof ridge with its mouth open. On both sides of the roof are equidistantly arranged green glaze beasts. An eye-catching "Prajna" plaque is placed under the roof in front of the main hall, black characters on a white background show no mundanity, and is full of aura in simplicity. The camel bells of the Silk Road are melodious, and the ultimate wisdom of "prajna" guarded by the ancient temple in the vicissitudes of life have quietly blended into the majestic smoke in great desert and magnificent sunset on the long river beyond the Great Wall.

25 玉泉寺
Yuquan Temple

早在南北朝后梁时期，梁宣帝敕建覆船山寺，即今天的"玉泉寺"。玉泉寺位于湖北省当阳市玉泉山东麓，因是佛教著名流派天台宗的发源地，使得颇多帝王贵胄亲自督造修建，李白、元稹、袁宏道等历代文人也留下了不少诗歌辞赋。古寺中各类殿堂楼阁林立，古迹众多。寺中的舍利宝塔最为精妙，精致玲珑却又坚固稳健，是我国现存最高、最重、最完整的一座古代铁塔。

与其他深藏于名山幽翠之中的古寺不同，玉泉寺周围几百亩的花海成团成簇，寺中的树叶也是五彩斑斓的。放眼望去，银杏、水杉、梧桐、香樟的树叶呈现出黄、棕、红、绿各色，与周围碧水相衬。

As early as the Houliang period of the Southern and Northern dynasties, Emperor Xuan built Fuchuanshan Temple, which is today's "Yuquan Temple". Yuquan Temple is located at the eastern foot of Yuquan Mountain in Dangyang City, Hubei Province. Because it is the birthplace of the famous Buddhist school Tiantai Sect, many emperors and nobles had personally supervised the construction. Li Bai, Yuan Zhen, Yuan Hongdao, and other literati also left a lot of poems and songs about it. There are many palaces and pavilions, as well as many historical sites in the ancient temple. The Stupa in the Temple is the most exquisite, sturdy, and stable. It is the tallest, heaviest, and most complete existing ancient iron tower in China.

Unlike other ancient temples that are hidden deep in the quiet and green mountains, the hundreds of acres of flowers around the Yuquan Temple are clustered, and even the leaves in the temple are colorful. Looking around, the leaves of ginkgo, metasequoia, phoenix tree, and camphor are in yellow, brown, red, and green colors, in contrast with the surrounding clear water.

26 天宁禅寺
Tianning Temple

天宁禅寺始建于唐贞观年间，位于江苏省常州市，前俯举世闻名的京杭大运河，后倚红梅公园。天宁禅寺无论晨昏四时皆是赏景佳期，清晨空灵，午后绚烂，黄昏苍茫。春日于此举目而望，观堤岸坡渚绿柳如丝。夏日凭栏倚坐，清风徐来，可纳微凉。秋日登塔远眺，梵铃清脆。冬日初雪，于萧瑟中赏白雪穿树作飞花。站在天宁宝塔高处，全城风貌皆收入眼中，胸中豪迈之情油然而生，浊气烦恼一扫而空。抄经祈福绕塔，此行心意正好。天宁宝塔梵音阁钟声响起，福音远播，四众弟子、十方檀越共同祈愿平安喜乐、善愿成就。

Tianning Temple was built during Zhenguan period of the Tang Dynasty and is located in Changzhou City, overlooking the world-famous Beijing-Hangzhou Grand Canal in front and leaning on Hongmei Park on back. Tianning Temple is a place worth visiting at any time of the day: clear morning, gorgeous afternoon, and gathering dusk. To appreciate the green willows on the embankment when watching from the temple in spring; to enjoy the cool breeze when leaning against a railing in summer; to listen to the clear bell ring when ascending the tower and looking into the distance in autumn; to admire the white snowflakes through the trees as flying flowers in the early snow in winter. Standing on the Tianning pagoda, one can overlook the whole city with boldness in heart and forget all the troubles and annoyances. It's right to copy the scriptures, pray in the temple and walk around the tower. When the bell in the Fanyin Pavilion of Tianning Pagoda is tolled, the gospels spread far away with disciples and benefactors jointly pray for peace and joy, and the accomplishment of good wishes.

27 大报恩寺
Dabao'en Temple

"南朝四百八十寺，多少楼台烟雨中"，杜牧这两句诗极言南朝时江南佛教文化之昌盛。而位于南京市秦淮区的大报恩寺，更是享誉中外。

大报恩寺历史悠久，其前身是孙吴时期的阿育王塔。该寺历经各朝，几经修缮，永乐年间，明成祖朱棣为报答父母——明太祖朱元璋和马皇后之恩，以皇宫规格重建，命名为"大报恩寺"。

大报恩寺的琉璃宝塔极其精美，集中国古代建筑艺术精华于一身。琉璃宝塔高达七八十米，通体琉璃，是当时中国最高的建筑，有"天下第一塔""南京瓷塔"之称，位列世界中古七大奇迹之一，更是当时中外人士游历南京的必到之处。每当夜幕降临，琉璃塔上就会点燃一百四十多盏佛灯，彻夜永明，为芸芸众生照亮未来的路。

"Among the four hundred and eighty temples built in the Southern dynasties, it's hard to count the number of them that look vaguely in the mist and rain" These two lines by Du Mu (a famous poet in the Tang Dynasty) accurately described the extreme prosperity of Buddhist culture during the Southern dynasties in south of the Yangtze River. The Dabao'en Temple, located in the Qinhuai District of Nanjing, is well-known both at home and abroad.

Dabao'en Temple has a long history, and it was originally the Ashoka Pagoda during the reign of Sun Quan in Wu State. The Temple went through various dynasties and was repaired several times. During the Yongle period, Emperor Chengzu (Zhu Di) of the Ming Dynasty, this temple was rebuilt according to the construction specifications of the royal palace and named "Dabao'en Temple" to repay the parents of Zhu Di, namely Emperor Zhu Yuanzhang and Queen Ma, for their kindness.

The Glazed Tower of Dabao'en Temple is extremely exquisite, integrating the essence of ancient Chinese architectural art. The Glazed Tower was seventy or eighty meters high as the tallest building in China at that time. It is known as the "No. 1 Tower in the World" and "Nanjing Porcelain Tower", ranked as one of the Seven Wonders of the Middle Ages in the world, and it was a must-visit place for Chinese and foreign visitors to Nanjing at that time. When night fell, more than one hundred and forty Buddha lamps would be lit on the Glazed Tower, shining through the night and illuminating the future for all living beings.

28 文殊院
Manjusri Monastery

　　成都的文殊院始建于隋，旧称"信相寺"。这里不但有精美且古老的佛教珍宝，也有风光旖旎的园林古建，平日不乏游人与信众。古寺皆为木构建筑，是典型的川西平原风格。寺内主要建筑依次坐落于正对山门的中轴线上，气势恢宏、巍峨壮观。寺内遍植名花奇卉，梅花、玉兰岁时争艳，千株银杏、香樟令人沉醉。千载间，鼎盛的香火带来的人气使这里的香园素斋成了本地知名的素食翘楚。文殊院内更荟萃了历代佛教珍宝，尤其是寺内供奉的三百余尊佛像。这些佛像的年代、材质、技艺各不相同，是研究中国佛教与中国雕塑艺术的珍贵资料。

　　The Manjusri Monastery in Chengdu was built in the Sui Dynasty and was formerly known as "Xinxiang Temple". There are not only exquisite and ancient Buddhist treasures, but also beautiful ancient gardens, and there is no shortage of tourists and believers on weekdays. The constructions in the ancient temple are all wooden buildings, which are typical of the west Sichuan Plain style. The main magnificent buildings in the temple are located on the central axis facing the mountain gate in turn. There are many famous flowers and plants in the temple. Plum blossoms and magnolias compete for beauty in blooming time. Thousands of ginkgo and camphor trees are attracting passers-by. For thousands of years, its popularity has even made the vegetation meal of Xiangyuan a well-known local vegetarian leader. There are Buddhist treasures from the past dynasties in the Manjusri Monastery, especially the more than 300 Buddha statues enshrined in the temple. These Buddha statues are of different ages, materials, and techniques. They are precious materials for studying Chinese Buddhism and Chinese sculpture art.

29 罗汉寺
Arhat Temple

　　罗汉寺坐落于重庆市中心最为繁华的解放碑地区，始建于北宋，千载间几番兴废，但寺内的古佛岩上依然存有四百余尊宋代摩崖石刻佛像。罗汉寺不似其他古寺藏于名山茂林，它屹立于闹市之中，仅仅用一道古老的墙便将空门梵音与俗世红尘分隔于两个世界。

　　罗汉寺的布局也与众不同，因山城这种特殊的地貌特征，无法像大多数传统寺庙那样拥有明显左右对称的中轴线，只能在尽量保持宗教建筑威严的同时，参考本地世俗园林和民居的特点，巧妙地利用地形，使寺庙营建与自然特征融为一体。因此，古老的罗汉寺具有了浓厚的川渝乡土建筑与景观的特点，多了点世俗的烟火气。也许从古至今，佛门清静与尘世欲望都只是一墙之隔……

　　Arhat Temple is located in the most prosperous Jiefangbei area in downtown Chongqing. Arhat Temple was built in the Northern Song Dynasty and has gone through ups and downs for thousands of years. However, there are still more than 400 Buddha statues carved on the rock in the Song Dynasty on the ancient Buddha rock in the temple. Unlike other ancient temples hidden in the famous mountains and forests, Arhat Temple stands in the downtown area with an ancient wall to separate the Buddhist world and the mundane world.

　　The layout of Arhat Temple is also unique. Because of the special geomorphic features of the mountainous city, the ancient temple cannot have an obvious left-right symmetrical central axis like most traditional temples. It can only try to maintain the majesty of religious buildings while referring to local secular characteristics of gardens and residential buildings to cleverly use the topography, integrating the temple construction and natural features. Therefore, the ancient Arhat Temple has the characteristics of strong local Sichuan-Chongqing architecture and landscape style with more secular vitalities. Perhaps since ancient times, Buddhist tranquility and earthly desires have always been separated just by a wall.

灵光寺
Lingguang Temple

　　北京市西山南麓的八大处，有一座古寺，始建于唐代，初名龙泉寺。辽代时，此处便已是皇家礼佛之处，明代重修后改称"灵光寺"，并沿用至今。寺庙几经兴废，八国联军侵入北京，灵光寺也未能幸免，建于辽代的招仙塔被炮火摧毁。僧人清理废墟瓦砾，在塔基中发现了装有释迦牟尼佛牙舍利的石函。中华人民共和国成立后，重修佛牙舍利塔，灵光寺也成为中外佛教徒朝拜的中心之一。

　　灵光寺佛牙舍利塔是十三层密檐塔格式，雕刻精巧，挺拔秀丽，神圣庄严。塔内的舍利堂中设置金刚座和彩绘屏风，以七宝金塔供奉佛牙舍利。寺中亭台楼阁、檐牙雕琢、曲径通幽、禅房花木，一点一滴皆是禅意，一丝一缕尽显佛心。灵光烁耀，佛牙永辉，名山古寺，远离尘世的喧嚣与嘈杂，以晨钟暮鼓透破禅关，因梵铃清脆心归净土。

　　There is an ancient temple at Badachu on the southern foot of West Mountain in Beijing. It was built in the Tang Dynasty and was originally named Longquan Temple. In the Liao Dynasty, this place was already a royal place for Buddha worship. After its rebuilding in the Ming Dynasty, it was renamed "Lingguang Temple" and is still in use today. The temple had gone through ups and downs. When the Eight-Power Allied Forces invaded Beijing, Lingguang Temple was not spared, and the Zhaoxian Pagoda built in the Liao Dynasty was destroyed. The monk cleaned up the rubble and found a stone box containing Shakyamuni's tooth relic in the base of the tower. After the founding of New China, the Buddha Tooth Stupa was rebuilt, and the Lingguang Temple became one of the worship centers for Buddhists in China and abroad.

　　The Buddha Tooth Stupa in Lingguang Temple is a thirteen-story multi-eaved pagoda with exquisite carvings, which is tall and beautiful, sacred and solemn. The relic hall in the tower is equipped with a vajra seat and painted screens, and a miniature seven treasures gold pagoda is used to enshrine the Buddha tooth relic. The buildings, the eaves, the lanes, and the flowers and trees in the temple are all endowed with the meaning of Zen and Buddhism. The shining light, the eternal Buddha tooth, and the temple in famous mountains are far away from the hustle and bustle of the world. The morning bell and the evening drum signify the thought of Zen, and the clear jingle bell leads the heart back to the pure land.

第三章
Chapter 3

觉悟人间
Quest for Spiritual Enlightenment

一 文化史上的名寺
Famous temples in the history of culture

栖霞寺
Qixia Temple

栖霞寺所处之山古时原有多个名字，但栖霞寺自建寺之后声誉日隆，梵烟不断，最终连这座漫山红枫的山也变作了"栖霞山"。

为了赏枫，千年来十多位古代帝王造访此地。乾隆皇帝六下江南五驻栖霞，可见对此间景色之钟情。寺外的红枫，寺内的金黄银杏，与秋日煦暖的阳光一起洒落在栖霞寺的每一个角落。

寺庙的梵音声声，香火缭绕。寺院倚山势而缓上，背倚千佛岩，四周层峦叠翠，万壑堆石，雄奇肃穆，气象万千。进山门拾级而上为弥勒殿、毗卢殿、法堂，最高处为藏经楼。依山势层层上升，格局严整美观。寺前有波平如镜的明镜湖和形如弯月的白莲池，远观蜿蜒起伏的山峰，耳目为之涤荡。

The mountain where Qixia Temple is located used to have several names. With the growing reputation and prosperity of Qixia Temple, the mountain full of red maple trees was gradually known as Qixia Mountain.

To appreciate the maple trees, more than ten emperors visited the area over the past thousands of years. Emperor Qianlong lived in Qixia five times during his six visits to the south of the Yangtze River Delta, which provides a glimpse of his favor for the scenery. Red maple leaves outside the temple and golden ginkgo leaves inside the temple are scattered on every corner of the temple in the warm autumn sun.

The smoke of incense rises in the chanting of Buddhist scriptures. The temple was constructed along the slope of the mountain with the Thousand Buddha Rock on its back and lush forests as well as rising peaks in the surrounding. When visitors go up along the steps, they will pass the mountain gate, the Maitreya Hall, the Pilu Hall, and the Dharma Hall, to the highest point, the Scripture Room. Rows of buildings are neatly arranged along the slope. In front of the temple, there is a mirror-like "Mirror Lake" and a white lotus pond in the shape of a crescent moon. Looking at the winding and undulating mountains in the distance from the lakes, visitors will find everything fresh and new.

02 国清寺
Guoqing Temple

国清寺又名至相寺,由静渊禅师始建于隋文帝开皇初年,是汉传佛教华严宗的发祥地。这里处在终南山北麓天子峪内,寺院高踞临岩,雄伟挺拔。寺前山峰如驼峰守望,寺后青山如青龙环抱,下有百泉汇流,负阴抱阳,瑞气葱葱,景色秀美。

从隋唐至今,这座千年古刹也曾香火鼎盛、佛光璀璨,也曾僧客星散、门庭冷落。历经风雨摧折,饱尝人间浩劫,有岁月流转的荣枯兴衰,亦有高僧苦心孤诣的修补重建。缭绕的香烟洗净俗世的思想,泛黄的经卷传递着幽深的禅意,惊醒了苦海迷梦人,唤回了世间功利客。在这里,山河大地、草木丛林皆是佛,一花一叶均可悟,烦恼妄想随风消逝,心不染半点尘埃。

Guoqing Temple, also known as Zhixiang Temple, was built by master Jingyuan during the reign of Emperor Wen of Sui. It is the birthplace and cradle of the Huayan school of Buddhism. Located in Tianziyu at the northern foot of Zhongnan Mountain, the magnificent temple is constructed on top of a cliff. Surrounded by lush green mountains and facing a river gathering water from springs, it boasts wonderful natural scenery.

From the Sui and Tang dynasties to the present, the thousand-year-old ancient temple has experienced its ups and downs in the vicissitudes of history. After weathering and destruction in bad times and the rebuilding by eminent monks with their painstaking efforts, the dreamer and the utilitarian are wakened in the swirling smoke of incense and the profound Buddhism embodied in the scriptures yellowish with time. Here, everything is relevant to Buddhas and can arouse enlightenment and drive away worries and distractions.

03 五祖寺
Wuzu Temple

五祖寺地处大别山主脉东端南沿，与九江隔江而望。该寺建于唐代永徽年间，是中国禅宗第五代祖师弘忍大师的道场，也是六祖惠能大师得法受衣钵之圣地，被御赐为"天下祖庭"。

千百年来，五祖寺晨钟暮鼓，梵音未停。寺中六棵千年青檀，沐浴过唐朝的阳光雨露，承受过宋朝的风霜雨雪，每一枚叶脉都传递着经卷里、岁月中的深深禅意。寂静山中，无论晴雨，不管春秋，无一不是"鸟鸣云间树，泉流涧底滩"的清幽意境。一花一世界，一叶一菩提，倘若不去流连世间的种种痴念，不再沾染凡尘的贪嗔，自然能够知足少虑，自然能够明月清风。

Located in the south of the east end of Dabie Mountain, Wuzu Temple is facing Jiujiang across the Yangtze River. The temple was built during the reign of Emperor Yonghui in the Tang Dynasty. It was the Ashram place for Master Hongren, the 5th Patriarch of Zen Buddhism. It was also where Master Huineng, the 6th Patriarch of Zen Buddhism, inherited his master's mantle. It was named by the emperor as "Tianxiazuting" (the Birthplace of all Buddhism temples).

For thousands of years through the Tang, Song, Yuan, Ming, and Qing dynasties, the morning bells, evening drums, and chanting of scriptures had never stopped. Six blue sandalwood trees of thousand-year-old had bathed in the sunshine and rain of the Tang Dynasty and withstood the wind and snow of the Song Dynasty. Every leaf vein conveys the profound Buddhism in the scriptures and the vicissitudes of times. The secluded mountains are always permeated with the tranquility characterized by "singing birds on the tree and running water in the springs" regardless of the weather and season. One can always "see a world in a wildflower and a bodhi in a leaf". Without the obsession with secular fallacy and greed, the feeling of deep contentment would be natural.

04 南华寺
Nanhua Temple

　　南华寺坐落于广东韶关的曹溪之畔，始建于南北朝，人称"东粤第一宝刹"。因禅宗六祖惠能在此弘法，也称六祖道场，是闻名遐迩的禅宗古寺。惠能在南华寺大倡顿悟法门，并主张不立文字，教外别传，直指人心，见性成佛。

　　古刹梵音，曹溪人静，水绕禅窗静，花开佛国香。南华禅寺的松月花鸟、清流白云、山林翠竹都是一道道清新自然的风景，犹如洗涤风尘的甘露，充盈着生命的感悟。宋代大文学家苏轼有诗赞曰："水香知是曹溪口，眼净同看古佛衣，不向南华结香火，此身何处是真依？"六祖真身像供奉在六祖殿内，他慈眉善目，神态安详，那淡定平和的目光，早已洞穿一切尘缘世事与人间冷暖。佛法在世间普渡芸芸众生，一点一滴皆是禅意，一丝一缕尽显佛心，万千姿态，终是悠远清明。

　　Located on the bank of Caoxi River in Shaoguan of Guangdong Province, Nanhua Temple was built in the Northern and Southern dynasties. It is reputed as the "No.1 Temple of Eastern Guangdong". As the most famous temple of Chan Buddhism, it is where Master Huineng, the 6th Patriarch of Chan Buddhism, once lived and taught. Master Huineng achieved sudden enlightenment in Nanhua Temple with the thought that enlightenment of the Buddha came not through intellectual reasoning, but rather through self-realization in Dharma practice and meditation.

　　The chanting of Buddhist scriptures is heard in the ancient temple beside the tranquil Caoxi River. Blooming flowers adds fragrance to the world of Buddha. Pines, the moon, flowers, birds, clear streams, white clouds, trees and bamboos, everything around the temple is refreshing and natural, like dewdrops that wash away the secular dust, arousing the enlightenment of life. Su Shi, a great litterateur in the Song Dynasty, wrote a poem to praise the temple, meaning that "It is by the fragrance of water in Caoxi River that we realize the arrival at the tranquil ancient temple. Where could true enlightenment be sought if we don't light incense in Nanhua Temple?" The real body of Master Huineng is enshrined in the Sixth Patriarch Hall. In a calm and peaceful demeanor, it seems that he had long seen through worldly matters. The promotion of Buddhism helps deliver all living creatures from torment. Every detail in the secluded temple with a long history presents the profound Chan Buddhism.

玄中寺
Xuanzhong Temple

玄中寺位于山西省交城县西北的石壁山上,因层峦叠嶂,山形如壁,故又名"石壁寺"。从北魏创寺至唐,一代高僧昙鸾、道绰、善导相继卓锡于此,使云中寺成为净土宗发祥地,由此,玄中寺千秋百代,一灯不灭,寺中保存有历代造像碑以及明代所建天王殿。穿行在玄中寺记忆的长廊中,依稀能够遥想出唐太宗李世民礼谒玄中寺时的盛况与庄严。玄中寺在烟火中日渐古朴,一草一木、一砖一瓦,都飘散着清净的韵味。游人凭栏而立,闻着檀香,洗尽内心的灰霾。

Xuanzhong Temple, also known as Shibi Temple, is built along the slope of the Shibi Mountain in the northwest of Jiangcheng County in Shanxi Province. From its founding in the Northern Wei Dynasty to the Tang Dynasty, eminent monks such as Tanluan, Daochuo, and Shandao resided in the temple and created the Pure Land Buddhism. Since then, Xuanzhong Temple has witnessed its ups and downs for thousands of years. The temple keeps buddha statues as well as Hall of Heavenly Kings built in the Tang Dynasty. Walking through the corridor in Xuanzhong Temple, visitors could imagine the grand and solemn ceremony when Emperor Taizong of the Tang Dynasty was visiting the temple. With the growing history of the temple, the charm of meditation and Buddhism has permeated every corner of it. Standing against the railings, all unpleasant feelings would be driven away in the smell of sandalwood.

普救寺
Pujiu Temple

"天下寺庙不谈情,唯有永济普救寺",元代王实甫的《西厢记》让这座始建于武则天时期的千年佛家古刹名扬海内外,张生与崔莺莺的爱情传奇给古寺增添了不少浪漫气息。此后的千载间,普救寺几经沧桑,起而复灭,灭而又起,不变的是一代又一代人对花好月圆的憧憬,正如山门所题楹联"普愿天下有情,都成菩提眷属"。

寺中殿宇楼阁,廊榭佛塔,依塬托势,逐级升高,给人以雄浑庄严、挺拔俊逸之感。寺内有座方形砖塔,原名舍利塔,俗称莺莺塔。不仅形制古朴、蔚为壮观,而且以奇特的结构、明显的回音效应著称于世。在塔侧以石叩击,塔上会发出清脆悦耳的蛙鸣之声,令人叹为观止。庭院深处,多少虔诚坚定的脚步在青石板上走过,怀着一颗清澈明净的心,来普救寺追寻那份夙世的因缘。

"Romance seldom happens in a temple except for Pujiu Temple in Yongji." The thousand-year-old ancient temple built during the rule of Wu Zetian in the Tang Dynasty gained far-reaching influence for *Romance of the Western Chamber* written by the Yuan Dynasty playwright Wang Shifu. The love legend between Zhang Sheng and Cui Yingying brought a sense of romance to the temple. In the following one thousand years, the temple had gone through ups and downs. Nevertheless, the yearning for a happy life, which is embodied in the couplet on the mountain gate meaning "may all romances end well under the Bodhi Tree", never changes from generation to generation.

The halls, pavilions, and pagodas are connected by corridors along the gradually rising terrain, making the whole building more imposing and magnificent. There is a square-shaped pagoda. Formerly known as the Sarira Dagoba, it is commonly called Yingying Pagoda. It is not only simple and magnificent but also famous for its peculiar structure and obvious echo effect. When the side of the tower is struck with a stone, the pleasant sound of frog croak would be heard. How amazing! In the depths of the courtyard, countless pious visitors and pilgrims have stepped over the bluestone road with firm belief and a clear mind in the pursuit of their destiny.

07 大相国寺
Daxiangguo Temple

　　大相国寺位于河南省开封市，据传寺址曾为战国四公子信陵君的故宅。这是一座中国人耳熟能详的古寺，北宋时期，相国寺深得皇家尊崇，多次扩建，是京城最大的寺院和全国的佛教活动中心。多少中国古代小说话本中，都不乏有关大相国寺的情节。而真实的历史中，大相国寺更是文豪名士的垂青之所，宋代黄庭坚、米芾、李清照夫妇俱是寺中常客。

　　古寺后因战乱烽火与黄河水患而衰落，清代重修后恢复了昔日的巍峨壮丽。大相国寺不仅遗存了八角琉璃殿、千手千眼佛等精美古迹，而且其梵音古乐也一脉绵延，至今不衰。每逢法会，梵音悠扬、仪仗威严，令观者仿佛穿越千年，重回风雅大宋。

　　Daxiangguo Temple is located in the Kaifeng City of Henan Province. It is said that the temple is the former residence of Lord Xinling, one of the "Four Lords of the Warring States". As a well-known temple in China, it was worshipped and respected by emperors of the Northern Song Dynasty and therefore reconstructed several times to become the largest temple in the imperial city and the center of Buddhism of the country. It frequently appeared in many ancient Chinese novels. In history, it was favored by many literati and celebrities, like Huang Tingjian (a famous calligrapher, painter, and poet in the Song Dynasty), Mi Fu (a famous painter, poet and calligrapher in the Song Dynasty), Li Qingzhao (a poet in the Song Dynasty) and her husband Zhao Mingcheng (a writer and scholar-official in the Song Dynasty), and so on.

　　After the decline due to wars and the flood of the Yellow River, it resumed its magnificence after being rebuilt in the Qing Dynasty. Not only historical relics like the hall with eight angles and color-glazed roof and the Avalokitesvara Bodhisattva have been well-preserved but also the ancient Sanskrit music has been passed down. On the occasion of the Buddhist ceremony, visitors would feel like traveling thousands of years back to the Song Dynasty in the melodious Sanskrit music and majesty honor guard team.

临济寺
Linji Temple

　　临济寺位于河北正定古城内，因靠近临济村而得名。古寺始建于东魏，兴盛于晚唐。晚唐时，一位传奇的高僧义玄禅师入驻此寺。这位高僧学识渊博，引来四方信徒纷纷来此拜师求学，由此，一支佛教禅宗流派——临济宗便在临济寺应运而生。后来，临济宗法脉东传，也成为了日本佛教主要宗派之一。临济寺历史悠久，因是临济宗的发祥地，每年世界各地有许多僧众信徒前来朝拜。

　　千载以来，临济寺几番兴废，然寺内的澄灵塔却始终屹立不倒。古塔高耸入云，华丽而巍峨，塔身雕有奇花异鸟、门窗户牖、莲花宝座，雕刻精细，匠心独具。层层塔身出檐深远，斗拱精巧，檐瓦脊兽皆为绿琉璃。于古城中遥遥望去，这座唐代古塔秀丽端庄，冥想间，心绪随宝塔飞入云间。

Located in the ancient city Zhengding in Hebei Province, Linji Temple got the name for its proximity to Linji Village. The ancient temple was established in the Eastern Wei Dynasty and became thriving in the late Tang Dynasty when a legendary eminent monk Yixuan settled in the temple. This knowledgeable monk attracted disciples from all over the country and thus created Linji school, one of the five major schools of Buddhism in China. Later, Linji school was introduced to Japan and became one of the major schools of Buddhism in Japan. As the cradle of Linji school, the ancient Linji Temple has attracted numerous pilgrims from all over the world.

Over thousands of years, the Linji Temple has experienced ups and downs, yet the Chengling Stupa stands firm in the temple. Towering into the sky, the stupa engraved with patterns of various flowers and birds on a lotus throne is of superb craftsmanship. The multi-eaves-style stupa has exquisite bracket sets and green glazed tiles and ridge animals. Looking from the distance in the ancient city, the stupa built in the Tang Dynasty is still elegant and dignified. Deep in meditation, the mind would soar into the sky with the stupa.

09 麓山寺
Lushan Temple

麓山寺位于湖南省长沙市岳麓山的山腰。麓山寺始建于西晋，随后佛事日弘，及至隋唐间高僧大德辈出，于湘江两岸盛极一时。文人名士也慕名而来，一代诗圣杜甫携游至此，也忍不住留下"寺门高开洞庭野，殿脚插入赤沙湖"这样气势磅礴的诗句。唐代书法家李邕撰文并亲书《麓山寺碑》以纪其胜。因其文章、书法、刻工俱佳，世称"三绝碑"。就这样，这座古寺进入了中国的文学史、书法史、艺术史。寺内僧众济济，塑像齐备，藏书丰富。殿堂掩映在层林叠翠之间，晨钟暮鼓，梵音悠扬，参观拜佛者络绎不绝，一派祥和、宁静的景象。

Lushan Temple is located halfway up the Yuelu Mountain in Changsha City of Hunan Province. It was built in the Western Jin Dynasty. Later, it attracted many eminent monks in the Sui and Tang dynasties and reached its heyday in the area along the Xiangjiang River. Many literati and celebrities came to the temple for its great fame. Du Fu, the "Poet-Sage", had visited the temple with his family and wrote the impressive lines meaning "The gate is wide open towards the boundless Dongting Lake and the foundation is deep-rooted in the Chisha Lake." Li Yong, a calligrapher in the Tang Dynasty, wrote an article to describe the scenery as the Lushan Temple Stele, which is reputed as the "Three Wonders Stele" for the excellent writing, calligraphy, and carving. In this way, this ancient temple entered the history of Chinese literature, calligraphy, and art. There are numerous monks, a diversity of statues, and a rich collection of books. The halls are hidden in the lush forest. In the morning bell, evening drums, and melodious Sanskrit music, the constant stream of visitors could feel the serene atmosphere.

开福寺
Kaifu Temple

　　开福寺位于湖南省长沙市的湘江之畔，始建于五代时期。悠悠千载间，围绕开福寺周边修建不绝，最终形成了环寺周围的紫微山、碧浪潮、白莲池、龙泉井、木鱼岭、拔禊亭、嘉宴堂、会春园、回步桥、舍茶亭等十六景。古寺内高树翠荫、碧水萦绕，引来无数文人高士吟诗作赋，"天然入画屏""花落满闲庭"等名句皆是为开福寺美景所作。

　　开福寺香火鼎盛于宋，彼时千僧云集，高僧辈出。日本僧人觉心也曾慕名而来，求法多时。觉心和尚回日本后卓锡日本纪州兴国寺，并受到龟山、后宇多两位日本天皇的重视。从此，开福寺法脉东传，与日本禅宗产生了一段不解之缘。

　　千载间，开福寺不仅法脉绵延不绝，文脉也源远流长。清末文人墨客与古寺诗僧成立"碧湖诗社"，在盈盈池水与花木扶疏间雅集会友，于清净庄严间悄然增添一缕绵长文脉。

Located on the bank of Xiangjiang River in Changsha City, Hunan Province, Kaifu Temple was built in the Five dynasties period. Over a thousand years, construction had been carried out around Kaifu Temple, and eventually, 16 landscapes are surrounding it, including Ziwei Hill, Blue Currents, White Lotus Pond, Longquan Well, Muyu Ridge, Baxi Pavilion, Jiayan Hall, Huichun Garden, Huibu Bridge and Shecha Pavilion. Towering trees and green shade and clean water winding in the temple attract countless literati and scholars to write poems here. "The temple is part of the natural landscape which is as beautiful as a painted screen" and "Falling flowers scatter about in the courtyard", these verses are written for picturesque landscapes of Kaifu Temple.

Kaifu Temple was in its heyday in the Song Dynasty when thousands of monks gathered in the temple and there were eminent ones among them. Japanese monk Juexin had also been attracted here to learn Dharma for a while. He stayed in Kokokuji Temple in Kishu, Japan, and converted Emperor Kameyama and Emperor Gouda. From then on, Kaifu Temple disseminated Dharma to Japan and was bound with Chan Buddhism there.

Over a thousand years, Kaifu Temple has not only handed down dharma-lineage through generations but also carried literature education. In the late Qing Dynasty, literati and monks of Kaifu Temple formed "Blue Lake Club" to gather with scholars and friends by the pond in flowers and trees, and quietly write more literary works in a peaceful and solemn environment.

归元寺
Guiyuan Temple

　　归元寺坐落在湖北省武汉市汉阳区翠微路西侧。"归元"出自佛经《楞严经》"归元无二路，方便有多门"。归元即归真，归于真寂本源的意思。

　　归元寺以建筑绝美、雕塑精妙、饶富珍藏而声名远播，以至于各国政要名流都曾探访于此。古寺有三重各具特色的庭院组成，古树参天，花木繁茂，泉清水甘，阳光透过朱漆窗棂，斑驳的光影于花间摇曳，满目皆是徽派建筑的清雅，满池的莲花与红锦鲤活跃灵动，却不损古寺之庄严。寺中罗汉堂的五百尊罗汉俱以传统夹纻技艺制成，高坐于台，于深邃宽阔的殿堂中依次有序排列，数目虽众却毫无拥挤之感，不由得让人感叹安排之精妙。于是"数罗汉"成了人们游罗汉堂的趣事。藏经阁中经书法器皆堪称稀有，安然居于古寺之中独守一方清净，远离俗世喧嚣。

Guiyuan Temple is located on the west of Cuiwei Road, Hanyang District, Wuhan City, Hubei Province. "Guiyuan" is derived from the Buddist chant "There is no other way to Guiyuan (nirvana), but many methods for practice" in Buddhist scripture *Śūraṅgama Sūtra*. Guiyuan means returning to nirvana, the original purity.

Guiyuan Temple is famous for its splendid architecture, exquisite sculpture, and a large number of treasures. Therefore, many politicians and celebrities all over the world have ever visited here. The ancient temple is composed of three courtyards with distinctive features, where there are towering trees, thriving plants, clear springs and water. Sunshine is through the red-painted windows and mottled lights dance among flowers. You may appreciate the elegance of Huizhou-style architecture here. Ponds of lotuses and lively red carps contrast with the solemn ancient temple. In Arhat Hall, 500 arhats are sitting on the platform, orderly arranged in the deep and wide hall. They are made by Jiazhu (hollowed mud sculpture) technique, large in amount but not crowded, making people can't help praising how wonderful the arrangement is. Therefore, counting of arhats becomes a funny activity in visiting Arhat Hall. Scriptures and instruments in the depositary of Buddhist texts are rare, stored in the ancient temple quietly and away from the clamor of the secular world.

12 清凉寺
Qingliang Temple

南京的清凉寺始建于南朝，自建寺以来，历遭毁废。清凉寺是佛教法眼宗的发源地，其禅学思想在中国佛教史上具有很高的地位和价值，影响远及日本、韩国及东南亚。

古寺所在的清凉山因寺而得名，随着清凉古寺名声日起，许多书院、文人居舍都汇集于此。金陵地区的文人隐士、贵胄名流燕居于此，日常与清凉寺僧人交游，在山间寺内谈经论诗、品茶赏画。这种博雅、圆融、多元的氛围使古寺兼具了宗教性与世俗性的双重文化魅力，因此"清凉问佛"成为了流传久远的"金陵四十八景"之一。即便跨越千年，如今的人们依然可以抛却世俗的繁杂与纷扰，在花木繁茂、浓荫蔽日的古寺之中得一片宁静。

Qingliang Temple in Nanjing was built in the Southern dynasties, and it has been damaged and abandoned many times since its establishment. As the cradle of Fayan School of Buddhism, its Zen Buddhism has high status and great value in the Buddhist history of China and influenced Japan, South Korea, and Southeastern Asian countries.

Qingliang Mountain is named after the ancient temple. When the temple is widely recognized, many academies and houses of literati were built around it. Scholars, hermits, nobles, and celebrities lived here, made friends, and traveled with monks of Qingliang Temple. They discussed Buddhism scriptures and poetry, tasted tea, and appreciated drawings. The atmosphere of erudition, harmony, and diversification endows the ancient temple with both religious and secular cultural charms. Therefore, "Learning Buddhist doctrines in Qingliang Temple" has become one of the "Forty-eight Interest of Jinling (ancient name of Nanjing)". Over a thousand years, people can still get rid of the complexity and disturbance of the world and find peace in the ancient temple with thriving plants and shading trees.

 **昭觉寺**
Zhaojue Temple

　　昭觉寺始建于唐贞观年间，唐僖宗取"以其昭昭使人昭，以其先觉觉后觉"之意，赐名"昭觉寺"。如今的古寺已被熙攘热闹的尘世高楼环绕，可一迈入古寺山门，满眼茂林秀木，清风徐来，斑驳的阳光树影随风摇曳。这般景致让多少古往今来的帝王才子念念不忘，清代的康熙皇帝在遥远的北京城中也曾心驰神往，遂留下了"入门不见寺，十里听松风"的畅想诗句。而近代艺术巨匠张大千在此寺一住四载之久，每日伴着晨钟暮鼓、渺渺炉香，画下多少传世之作。昭觉寺在古人的记载中素有"伙食丰洁，法食华焕"的美誉，因此于茶室或斋堂中品一盏清茶、尝一碗素斋，更可让人情愿将清静时光尽数消磨于古寺，浑然忘却古寺一墙之外的喧闹俗世。

Zhaojue Temple was built in Zhenguan Period in the Tang Dynasty. Emperor Xizong of the Tang Dynasty named it "Zhaojue Temple" according to phrases in *The Book of Mencius* that "The sage is wise enough to make others understand and he is awakened to enlighten others." Nowadays, such an ancient temple has been surrounded by skyscrapers and the bustling and hustling world. However, you can still see thriving trees, feel the breeze and look at the mottled sunshine and swaying shadow of trees when you step into the temple. Bearing in minds of emperors and gifted scholars through the ages, the landscape made Emperor Kangxi in the Qing Dynasty yearned for it and he wrote, "Pass through the gate, you cannot see the temple, but hear the song of pine trees in ten miles when they are swayed by the breeze." Modern artist Zhang Daqian has lived here for 4 years. With morning bell rings, evening drumbeats and smoking incenses, he drew many paintings to be handed down through generations. Zhaojue Temple was praised in the records of ancient scholars as "Rich and clean in meals and brilliant and resplendent in Buddhist practice". Therefore, taste a cup of tea or a bowl of vegetarian foods, making people willing to spend their time in the peaceful ancient temple and forget the clamorous world on the other side of the wall.

第四章
Chapter 4

溪花禅意
Zen in the Spring and Flowers

一 名山胜景中的古寺
Ancient temples in famous mountains and scenic spots

01 灵隐寺
Lingyin Temple

　　灵隐寺又名云林寺,始建于东晋咸和元年,是中国佛教禅宗十大古刹之一。灵隐寺端坐在西湖以西的灵隐山麓,透过西湖云烟缥缈的雾霭与烟水,拨开飞来峰与冷泉低垂的帘幕,就来到了这座幽雅秀丽的仙山佛国。

　　"溪山处处皆可庐,最爱灵隐飞来孤",这是苏轼笔下秀峰辉映、古木茂盛的灵隐寺。穿越一千六百多年的时光,魏晋的烟火依稀在昨天萦绕,唐宋的禅韵似乎仍笼罩着整座古寺,明清悠悠回荡的钟鼓声仿佛还在唤醒迷失的今人。灵隐寺在西湖的群峰林泉中,虽经受时间沧桑的变迁,一怀风骨却不改当年。

　　Lingyin Temple, also known as Yunlin Temple, was built in the first year of the Xianhe period in the Eastern Jin Dynasty. It is one of the ten ancient Zen Buddhist temples in China. Lingyin Temple sits at the foothills of Lingyin Mountain to the west of the West Lake. Passing through the misty water of the West Lake, the lush forests of Feilai Peak, and the running cold spring, you come to this elegant and beautiful fairy Buddhist Mountain.

　　"Among all the livable mountains and streams, I love Lingyin Mountain and Feilai Peak the most" is used by Su Shi to describe the Lingyin Temple with beautiful peaks and lush ancient trees. Through more than 1,600 years, you can still peep at the traces of the life in Wei and Jin dynasties, feel the lingering charm of Zen of Tang and Song dynasties, and hear the bells and drums of the Ming and Qing dynasties echoing in the temple to awaken the fascinated visitors. Hidden in the peaks and springs of the West Lake, Lingyin Temple still keeps its strong character although it has withstood the vicissitudes of time.

02 天童寺
Tiantong Temple

  天童寺是佛教禅宗名寺，号称"东南佛国"。寺院坐落在层峦叠嶂的太白山下，"群峰抱一寺，一寺镇群峰"，寺周群峰叠翠，苍松如海，青竹连片，峻石幽谷，溪泉流漱。自西晋永康年间义兴祖师开山以来，天童寺经历代相承，终成巍巍卓立的十方丛林。殿宇金碧辉煌，庄严气派，规模之恢宏，建筑之精美，为国内鲜见。

  天童寺与日本禅宗关系密切，日本曹洞宗尊天童寺为祖庭。日本历史上著名的"画圣"雪舟和尚也曾在寺中参禅，将天童寺中那出入于群山松涛的真自然，怀抱禅律的逸气尽展现于他的作品中，因此被明宪宗赞为"天童第一座"。时光流转，虔诚地走过万松大道，来到天童禅寺的礼佛者仍可感受那洗涤凡尘的意境与深意。

Tiantong Temple is a famou temples in Chan Buddhism, and is called "Buddhist Kingdom in the Southeast". This temple is located in the Taibai Mountain with rising layers of ridges. The line of "a temple in the peaks is the soul of the peaks" is used to describe the verdant peaks with lush pines, green bamboos, steep valleys, and running streams and springs where the temple is located. Since the founding of the temple in the mountain by Yixing Patriarch in the Yongkang period of the Western Jin Dynasty, Tiantong Temple has been passed down through generations and eventually became an admirable famous Buddhist temple. It is rare to see such a magnificent temple hall in such a large scale and exquisite architecture in China.

Tiantong Temple is closely related to Japanese Chan Buddhism, and the Japanese Soto Zen believes that Tiantong Temple is its ancestral court. Toyo Sesshu, the famous "painting saint" in Japanese history, had once practiced Zen meditation in the temple and demonstrated the true nature of Tiantong Temple among the mountains and pines and the elegant spirit of embracing the laws of Zen in his paintings. Therefore, Emperor Xian of the Ming Dynasty once praised Sesshu as "the chief monk of Tiantong". As time goes by, the Buddhist worshipers who come to Tiantong Temple along Wansong Avenue religiously can still feel the artistic conception and profound meaning of washing off the secular thoughts.

03 九华山寺庙群
Jiuhua Mountain Temple Complex

　　九华山有"莲花佛国"之称,以地藏菩萨道场驰名天下。连绵山峰形成的天然睡佛,成为自然景观与佛教文化有机融合的典范。境内群峰竞秀,九十九座寺庙形成独具特色的寺庙群,晨钟暮鼓,梵音袅袅,有僧尼近千人,佛像万余尊。

　　化城寺是九华山开山祖寺,被视为地藏菩萨化身的金乔觉渡海来唐,便是在这里卓锡,苦心修行七十五载,化城寺也因此成为九华山寺院的"总丛林"。百岁宫亦称"十方丛林",内有五百罗汉堂供奉五百尊罗汉,气势壮观。祇园寺大雄宝殿内有三尊喷金大佛,在九华山寺庙群中堪称翘楚。甘露寺周围古木参天,深藏万松之中。肉身宝殿、天台寺、慧居寺、天池庵……处处玄妙灵秀,果然如诗仙李白所言:"妙有分二气,灵山开九华。"

　　Jiuhua Mountain is known as the "Buddhist Kingdom of Lotus" and is famous all over the world as the Ashram for Ksitigarbharaja. The natural sleeping Buddha formed by the continuous mountain peaks has become a model of the organic integration of natural landscape and Buddhist culture. Among the peaks in the area, 99 temples form a unique temple complex with nearly a thousand monks and nuns, and more than ten thousand Buddha statues there bathed in morning bells and evening drums, as well as the chanting of Sanskrit.

　　Jin Qiaojue, who is regarded as the incarnation of Ksitigarbharaja, crossed the sea to China in the Tang Dynasty. He cultivated in Huacheng Temple for seventy-five years, and the temple thus becomes the "General Buddhist monastery" of Jiuhua Mountain temple complex. The Temple of Long Live is also known as the "Ten-direction Complex". A magnificent "Hall of Five-hundred Arhats" enshrining five hundred Arhats is in the palace. There are three gold-sprayed Buddhas in the Mahavira Hall in the Qiyuan Temple, which is among the best statues in Jiuhua Mountain Temple Complex. The Ganlu Temple is surrounded by towering ancient pine trees. Roushen Hall (Hall of Buddhist mummies), Tiantai Temple, Huiju Temple, Tianchi Nunnery … these temples are mysterious and beautiful, just as the poet Li Bai wrote, "The mystery of yin and yang is found in the nine Lian-shaped (lotus-shaped) peaks of this holy mountain."

04 惠山寺
Huishan Temple

　　惠山寺为"南朝四百八十寺"之一,古木参天,梵宇重重,鸟语花香,是一个清净庄严的伽蓝圣地。惠山寺是禅宗道场,文化底蕴格外深厚,诗文碑刻甚佳。"云山相照翠会合,殿阁对走凉参差。"古往今来,多少骚人墨客甚至帝王将相巡游江南水乡时,都要在惠山寺探访参禅,为之留下了无数诗句墨宝。

　　浮生逆旅虽难堪破,但梵宇慈云亦让人心有所悟。庙宇巍然,楼阁精巧,大好林泉可入画;溪山依旧,云卷云舒,无边禅意得真如。佛珠渗透出古木馨香,虽可略开尘眼识烟霞,但无奈劳生未了。不知多年后星移斗转,这古刹深处的风又会吹拂谁的衣衫。

Huishan Temple is one of the "Four hundred and eighty temples built in the South dynasties" and a pure and solemn sangha-arama Holy Land with towering ancient woods, numerous halls, and palaces, as well as birds and flowers. Huishan Temple is a temple of Zen Buddhism with profound cultural heritage and excellent poems and inscriptions, such as "the cloud and the mountain meet in the green trees; the cool breeze is through split-leveled halls and pavilions". Throughout the ages, many literati and even emperors and officials have visited the Huishan Temple for cultivation and left their poems and calligraphy about the temple when they were traveling in the Yangtze River Delta.

Although life is tough, the solemn religious concepts may bring people epiphany. The majestic temple, the exquisite pavilion, and beautiful natural sceneries are good materials for painting. The same mountains and streams in the passing time just represent the true meaning of Zen. The Buddha beads permeate the fragrance of ancient woods, which slightly shows the ecstasy of Buddhism, however, people have to suffer in the secular world before going to the other world. After many years in the future, who will stand here to feel the wind blowing from the depth of this ancient temple?

悬空寺
Hanging Temple

　　悬空寺建于北魏后期，是国内现存最早、保存最完好的古代高空木构摩崖建筑，也是中国仅存的佛、道、儒三教合一的独特寺庙。悬空寺上方是危危巨岩的翠屏峰，下方是水流湍急的金龙峡。雕梁画栋的层层楼阁奇迹般地挂在悬壁之上，像一幅玲珑剔透的浮雕，镶嵌在万仞峭壁间，颇有"上延霄客，下绝嚣浮"之感。大诗人李白游览悬空寺后，在石崖上挥笔书写了"壮观"二字。

　　层层楼阁，凌空危挂。经历过一千五百余年的风霜，悬空寺看尽了王朝更替。人来人往，云起云落，它在战乱天灾中屡经修葺，依然矗立在绝壁之上细数着沧桑，与时间同流。

　　Built in the late Northern Wei Dynasty, Hanging Temple is the earliest and best-preserved high-altitude wooden cliff building in China. It is also the only existing temple that combines Buddhism, Taoism, and Confucianism in China. Above the Hanging Temple is the Cuiping Peak with the precipitous huge rocks, and below is the fast-flowing Golden Dragon Gorge. The numerous layers of pavilions of carved beams and paintings are miraculously hung on the overhanging cliff, like an exquisite and translucent relief inlaid among the cliffs, bringing a feeling of "going up to the heaven to meet the deities and forget all the tedious annoyances in life". After visiting the Hanging Temple, the great poet Li Bai wrote two Chinese characters of "Zhuang Guan" (spectacular) on the cliff.

　　In more than 1,500 years, Hanging Temple has witnessed the change of dynasties with its numerous layers of pavilions hanging on the overhanging cliff. This temple has been repaired several times in wars and natural disasters, while it is still standing on the cliff to watch people coming and going and the clouds rising and falling.

06 永祚寺
Yongzuo Temple

永祚寺俗称双塔寺，始建于明朝万历年间。这是一座全部由砖仿木无梁建筑组成的寺院，在中国古建筑群中极为罕见。据传，寺内的文峰塔、舍利塔建成后，太原的文章圣手层出不穷，故这两座塔被誉为"文笔双峰"。双塔巍峨俊秀，直插云天，屹立在晋阳大地之上。

　　双塔雄伟挺立，傲视古今，在明代风起云涌时拔地而起，历经烟火冲洗，惯看王朝兴替，依然携一身仙风灵气栖于古刹。牡丹、墨宝与双塔并称永祚寺"三绝"。寺中牡丹种类繁多，最可贵的是数十株明代紫霞仙牡丹，经历了数百个春秋，虽老干虬枝，却仍苍劲旺盛，花朵硕大如盘，馨香浓郁。寺内的古碑集清以前各代著名书法大家的墨宝于一堂，有真、草、隶、篆各种书体，无一不有。这些心性迥异的笔墨参透着浓淡不同的人生感悟，与永祚寺流传千古。

Yongzuo Temple, commonly known as the Twin Pagoda Temple, was built during the Wanli period of the Ming Dynasty. This is a beamless temple entirely composed of wood-like bricks, which is extremely rare in Chinese ancient buildings. According to legend, after the completion of the Wenfeng Pagoda and the Stupa in the temple, many literary masters appeared in Taiyuan city, so these two pagodas are known as the "Two peaks of Paper and Brush Pen". The two majestic pagodas are pointing straightly into the sky and standing in the city of Jinyang (ancient name for Taiyuan).

These two pagodas rose high during the turbulent times of the Ming Dynasty and still stand in the ancient temple after experiencing the rises and falls of dynasties. The peony, calligraphy works, and the two pagodas are collectively called the "three treasures" of Yongzuo Temple. There are many kinds of peonies in the temple, and the most valuable are dozens of "Zixiaxian" peonies planted in the Ming Dynasty. After hundreds of years, the plate-like flowers are vigorously blooming with attractive fragrance on the ancient rough branches. The ancient steles in the temple gathered the calligraphy works of many famous calligraphy masters of all dynasties before the Qing Dynasty. There are all kinds of scripts: Zhen script, running script, official script, and seal script. These calligraphy works of different features represent different insights into life and have been passed down through the ages with Yongzuo Temple.

07 塔院寺
Tayuan Temple

塔院寺是五台山著名的五大禅处之一，因院内有高耸入云的大白塔而得名。作为五台山的标志，大白塔拔地而起，在红墙、琉璃瓦殿顶的陪衬下，显得巍峨壮观。塔的垂檐和束腰上均挂有风铃，全塔上下共有风铃二百五十二个。风吹铃动，叮当作响，大白塔古韵犹存，禅味悠远，在超然逸世的空灵韵致中，感悟菩提的心境和莲花的慈悲。

大白塔东侧还有高两丈余的砖构文殊发塔，相传文殊菩萨显圣遗留的金发就藏在其中。五台山作为文殊菩萨的道场，流传着众多文殊显圣的传说，也留存了无数得道高僧的明月清风，承载着无数香客的匆匆步履。

Tayuan Temple is one of the five famous Buddhist places in Wutai Mountain. It is named after the Great White Pagoda in the courtyard. As a symbol of Wutai Mountain, the Great White Pagoda rises from the ground and looks majestic against the backdrop of the red walls and glazed tile roof. Wind chimes are hung on the eaves and waist of the pagoda. There are 252 wind chimes on the whole pagoda. The blowing wind and the jingling bells are telling the ancient charm and the Zen flavor of the Great White Pagoda, and make people feel the mind of Bodhi and the compassion of lotus in the ethereal charm of transcendence.

On the east side of the Great White Pagoda, there is also a two-fathom-tall brick Manjusri Tower. According to legend, the blond hair left by Manjusri Bodhisattva's manifestation is preserved in it. As the Ashram of Manjusri Bodhisattva, Wutai Mountain has many legends about Manjusri sacred manifestation, retains the noble deeds of countless enlightened eminent monks, and bears the hasty steps of countless pilgrims.

08 外八庙
Eight Outer Temples

外八庙是河北承德避暑山庄东北部八座藏传佛教寺庙的总称，由溥仁寺、溥善寺（现已不存）、普宁寺、安远庙、普陀宗乘之庙、殊像寺、须弥福寿之庙、广缘寺八座寺庙组成，是世界上独一无二的宗教建筑群和中国古建筑艺术的巅峰之作。

外八庙建筑群规模雄伟宏大，重檐攒尖，鎏金铜瓦，法铃宝顶，檀香袅袅。远视鎏金闪光，辉煌壮观；近看红白相映，庄严秀丽，一片人间净土之感。这里的古寺多仿塞外名寺而建，凝聚了西藏布达拉宫的气势、日喀则扎什伦布寺的雄奇、山西五台山殊像寺的风采、新疆伊犁固尔扎庙的华丽，还可以看到世界最大的木制佛像千手千眼观世音菩萨，可谓多民族建筑艺术和文化交融的典范。

"Eight Outer Temples" is the general name of the eight Zang Buddhist temples in the northeast of Chengde Mountain Resort of Hebei Province. It consists of Puren Temple, Pushan Temple (no longer existing), Puning Temple, Anyuan Temple, Temple of the Potaraka Doctrine, Shuxiang Temple, Temple of Sumeru Fushou, and Guangyuan Temple, which is a unique religious building complex in the world and the pinnacle of Chinese ancient architectural art.

The scale of the building complex is magnificent, with multi-layer eaves and pyramidal roofs, gilded bronze tiles, ceilings with the picture of bells, and sandalwood fragrance. Seen from the distance, these temples are showered in gilt golden light; with a closer look, red and white colors reflect each other, representing a solemn, beautiful, pure paradise on earth. Ancient temples here were mostly built after their famous counterparts beyond the Great Wall. They preserve the momentum of the Potala Palace in Xizang, the majesty of the Tashilhunpo Monastery in Shigatse, the style of the Shuxiang Temple in Wutai Mountain of Shanxi, the gorgeousness of the Ghulja Temple in Ili of Xinjiang, and admire the largest wooden Buddha statue of Avalokitesvara with thousand-hand and thousand-eye in the world. It's the model of the integration of multi-ethnic architectural art and culture of Han, Mongolia, and Zang.

09 天门山寺
Tianmenshan Temple

　　天门山寺是湘西地区的佛教中心，始建于明朝，现已原址重建，采用清代官式风格，三进两殿，气势浩大。寺内存放一枚尼泊尔蓝毗尼中华寺赠予的释迦牟尼佛舍利，这是中国仅有的五枚之一。

　　天门山寺坐落在天门山上，有一山独尊的气概。徜徉于古刹，殿宇罗列，曲径通幽，秀丽的山色令人怡悦。于浓荫蔽日的参天古木间，窥见时光的流逝；于造型奇巧的观音阁中，以缭绕的香烟洗净俗世思想，心神不染半点尘埃……深山古寺便是如此古雅清幽，于树影婆娑下感受风吹过的韵味，品味茶香飘过的禅趣。

Tianmenshan Temple is the center of Buddhism in the western Hunan region. It was built in the Ming Dynasty and was rebuilt today on the original site. It adopts the official style of the Qing Dynasty, with three courtyards and two halls, showing a grand scale. Stored in the temple is a relic of Buddha Shakyamuni gifted by the Lumbini Chinese temple in Nepal, which is one of only five in China.

The Tianmenshan Temple is located on Tianmen Mountain as the dominator of the mountain. It's pleasant to wander in the ancient temple, enjoying the halls along the winding lanes and the beautiful mountain scenery. Visitors can feel the passage of time in the towering ancient woods that shade the sun, wash off the secular thoughts with smoky incense in the intricately shaped Avalokitesvara pavilion. It's so quaint and quiet to feel the charm of the wind and taste the Zen in the fragrance of tea in this ancient temple.

10 金山寺
Jinshan Temple

金山寺始建于东晋，是中国佛教诵经设斋、礼佛拜忏和追荐亡灵的水陆法会的发源地。金山寺布局依山就势，殿宇栉比，亭台相连，遍山布满金碧辉煌的建筑，山与寺融为一体，以至于无法窥见山的原貌，因而有"金山寺裹山"之说。

白蛇水漫金山的传说，梁红玉击鼓战金山的故事，都在这里酝酿生长。苏东坡与主持佛印曾在这里吟诗作画，论公案、打机锋……时光沧桑，风云已改，人事已非，金山寺那悠然的禅意、无边的佛法，似乎可以贯穿古今，普度生灵。那昼夜流淌不息的扬子江水沉淀着历史的厚重，淘尽凡尘的聚散悲欢。

Jinshan Temple was built in the Eastern Jin Dynasty and is the birthplace of the rituals of chanting and fasting, worshipping and confessing, and Shuilu Puja for expiating the sins of the dead in Chinese Buddhism. The layout of the Jinshan Temple follows the ridges of the mountain. The closely arranged halls and the connected pavilions are built on the mountain and integrated with the mountain, so it's hard to tell the original appearance of the mountain. Therefore, the words "the Jinshan Temple is covering the mountain" are used to describe this scene.

The legends of "Bai Suzhen flooding the Jinshan Temple" and "Liang Hongyu beating drums to cheer the army at the battlefield of Jinshan" all originated from here. Su Dongpo and the abbot Buddha Yin used to recite poems and draw paintings, discuss public cases, and have witty chats ... As time goes by, the artistic Zen and boundless Buddhist spirit of Jinshan Temple seem to be able to run through ancient and modern times and save lives. The Yangtze River, which flows day and night, accumulates the weight of history, gathering all the mundane sorrows and joys.

镇国寺
Zhenguo Temple

　　镇国寺位于名城高邮,是京杭大运河上一颗璀璨的明珠。寺庙始建于唐代,诸朝对寺院皆有修葺,规模甚伟,气势恢宏,香火鼎旺。然年深日久,饱经沧桑,庙宇僧寮毁损殆尽,唯存遗址及千年唐塔,风韵不改当年。

　　有"南方大雁塔"之称的镇国寺塔临水而居,保留了唐骨明风的建筑特色。在烟火里悟禅味,于流水中听梵音,有明月晓风轻拂,有古岸垂柳相伴,过往的历史,还有散落的文明,在山水中缄默不语,成为了一份出尘的守望。此岸是烟云琼花的无尽梦境,彼岸是暮鼓晨钟的清醒禅意。

Zhenguo Temple, located in the famous city Gaoyou, is a shining pearl on the Beijing-Hangzhou Grand Canal. The temple was built in the Tang Dynasty and was repaired in all the following dynasties. It has a large scale, magnificent momentum, and is frequented by visitors. Although most buildings in the temple had been destroyed, the remaining relics and the pagoda built in the Tang Dynasty have kept their original flavor.

The pagoda of Zhenguo Temple, known as the "Southern Big Wild Goose Pagoda", is built by the river, retaining the architectural features of the Tang and Ming dynasties. Zen in normal life, Sanskrit in running water, the bright moon and tender wind, the bending willows along the water bank, as well as the history and the scattered civilization are surrounding us. The ancient temple is watching the world in silence. The endless dream of misty clouds and jade flowers of secular life is facing the sober Buddhist paradise of morning bell and evening drum.

12 灵岩山寺
Lingyanshan Temple

灵岩山寺位于江苏省苏州市太湖之滨，春秋时是吴王夫差为西施所建的馆娃宫。东晋时，司空陆玩曾居于灵岩山，因得闻佛法，故舍宅为寺，成为灵岩道场之开端。20世纪30年代，净土宗第十三祖师印光法师于原址重建，并将其改为"灵岩山寺"。在唐宋元明清几代，灵岩山寺皆为江南名寺。

在秀绝冠江南的灵岩山麓有此胜境，它既是钟灵毓秀的大美自然，又是普度众生的无上菩提。在岁月的回眸里，在古刹深沉的肃穆中，听远处历史的回音，用禅意的那份淡定涤荡心灵的尘埃。

Lingyanshan Temple is located on the shore of Taihu Lake in Suzhou City, Jiangsu Province. It was Guanwa Palace built by King Fuchai of Wu State for Xi Shi (one of the four renowned beauties in ancient China) in the Spring and Autumn Period. In the Eastern Jin Dynasty, Sikong Luwan once lived in Lingyan Mountain. Because he learned about Buddhism here, his house was then used as a temple and became the original place of Lingyan Ashram. In the 1930s, Master Yinguang, the 13th ancestor of the Jingtu Zong (The Pure Land School of Buddhism), rebuilt it on the original site and renamed it as "Lingyanshan Temple". In the Tang, Song, Yuan, Ming, and Qing dynasties, the Lingyanshan Temple was a famous one in south of the Yangtze River.

This wonderful place at the foothill of Lingyan Mountain which is the most beautiful place in the Yangtze River Delta is both equipped with natural beauty and a Buddhist place for universal salvation. Looking back the past years, the dust in the heart can be washed away with the calmness of Zen in the deep solemnity of the ancient temple and the echo of the distant history.

13 大召寺
Dazhao Temple

大召寺汉名原为"弘慈寺",是万历皇帝赐名,清代皇太极将其改为"无量寺"。因寺内供奉一座银佛,又称"银佛寺"。这尊银佛是全国最大的释迦牟尼银佛像,铸造于明代,高三米,用纯银三千斤。

大召寺是呼和浩特最早建成的黄教寺院,在当地有广泛的影响。中原博大的文化、灿烂的佛光散落在塞外这片土地上,滋生出了精深思想的繁花。无数的寺院高僧,无数的佛教圣徒,在荒野的古道上行走,探寻着深邃的古老文化,也拾取了灿烂的佛学经典。

Dazhao Temple was formerly known as "Hongci Temple", which was bestowed by Emperor Wanli, and was renamed "Wuliang Temple" by Emperor Hong Taiji of the Qing Dynasty. Because a silver Buddha is enshrined in the temple, it is also called "Silver Buddha Temple". This 3-meter-high silver Buddha is the largest silver Buddha statue of Shakyamuni in China, which was cast in the Ming Dynasty with three thousand *jin* of pure silver.

Dazhao Temple is the earliest temple of Gelug School built in Hohhot, which has a far-reaching influence in the Mongolian area. The extensive culture of the Central Plains and the splendid Buddhist thoughts are spread to land outside the Great Wall, breeding flowers of profound thoughts. Countless eminent monks and countless Buddhist saints were walking on the ancient road in the wilderness, exploring the profound ancient culture, and also picking up the brilliant Buddhist classics.

14 五当召
Wudang Lamasery

蒙古语"五当"意为"柳树","召"为"庙宇"之意。五当召始建于清康熙年间,是第一世活佛罗布桑加拉措以西藏扎什伦布寺为蓝本兴建的。它与西藏的布达拉宫、青海的塔尔寺和甘肃的拉卜楞寺齐名,是中国藏传佛教的四大名寺之一。

寺庙为平顶梯状方形楼,是传统的藏式建筑,在群山环抱之下尤显雄浑壮观。远远望去,这座庞大的古建筑群透着一种博大的胸襟和超凡的力量,让人心生景仰。行走在梵音冲洗过的道路,古刹的色调变得斑驳,然而这种斑驳依旧绮丽,并随着似水流年成为大漠风沙中的一抹亮色。

In the Mongol language, "Wudang" means "willow tree", and "Zhao" means "temple". Wudang Lamasery was built during the Kangxi period of the Qing Dynasty. It was built by the first living Buddha, Rob Sanggalatso, after the model of the Tashilhunpo Temple in Xizang. It is as famous as the Potala Palace in Xizang, the Ta'er Lamasery in Qinghai, and the Labrang Monastery in Gansu, and is one of the four famous temples of Zang Buddhism in China.

The temple is a flat-topped ladder-shaped square building, a traditional Zang architecture, which is majestically surrounded by mountains. Seen from a distance, this huge group of ancient buildings reveals a broad mind and extraordinary power, which makes people admire. Walking on the road washed by the Sanskrit, the color of the ancient temple becomes mottled, but this mottle is still beautiful and becomes a bright color in the desert with passing time.

15 布达拉宫
Potala Palace

布达拉宫是现存海拔最高的宫殿,最初是吐蕃王朝赞普松赞干布为迎娶文成公主而兴建的。它依山垒砌,同山体融合在一起,宫墙红白相间,宫顶金碧辉煌,群楼重叠,殿宇嵯峨,气势雄伟,有横空出世、气贯苍穹之势。

布达拉宫是雪域高原上最神圣的宫殿,也是所有朝圣者心中的圣地。它有唐宋元明清的烟火痕迹,有先贤上师们的诵经之声,亦有千年以来凝聚的精神信仰。经幡在风中飘摇,转经筒被时光浸泡,翻阅古老的经卷,或可超凡脱世。光阴须臾,行客匆匆,山依然巍峨,布达拉宫庄严如故……

Potala Palace is the existing palace with the highest altitude, which was originally built by the Tubo btsan po Songtsen Gampo for his marriage with Princess Wencheng. The Potala Palace is built on the hillside and merged with the mountain. The red-white wall palace is magnificent with a golden roof and multi-layer buildings.

The Potala Palace is the most sacred palace on the snow-covered plateau and is also a holy place in the hearts of all pilgrims. It has life traces from the Tang, Song, Yuan, Ming, and Qing dynasties, the sound of chanting by the sage masters, and the spiritual beliefs that have been condensed for thousands of years. The prayer flags were swaying in the wind, the prayer wheels were soaked in. One may have been enlightened, by scanning the ancient scriptures. Time is short; visitors are in a hurry; the mountains are still majestic; and the Potala Palace is as solemn as ever …

16 塔尔寺
Ta'er Lamasery

　　塔尔寺位于青海省西宁市湟中区城区。明朝洪武年间,在这里修建了一座塔,名叫"莲聚塔",后来围绕着这座塔,建起了一座座禅堂佛殿,高低错落,交相辉映,气势壮观。因先有塔后有寺,故而又名"塔尔寺"。

　　塔尔寺是藏传佛教格鲁派创始人宗喀巴大师的诞生地,也是西北地区的佛教中心之一。碧彻丹楹前面飘着一排排经幡,殿宇内千百盏酥油灯闪烁着淡红色的火焰,这是一个庄严华丽的净土世界。佛法无边照古今,虔诚的信徒朝拜古老的庙宇,敲扣深掩的重门,在佛陀的世界寻觅心灵的慰藉。

Ta'er Lamasery is located in the downtown area of Huangzhong District, Xining City, Qinghai Province. During the Hongwu period of the Ming Dynasty, a pagoda called "Lianju" was built here. Later, numerous meditation halls and Buddha rooms were built around this pagoda. It became a majestic multi-layer building complex and was then named "Ta'er Lamasery".

Ta'er Lamasery is the birthplace of Lama Tsong Khapa, the founder of the Gelug school. It is also one of the many centers of Buddhism in the Northwest. There are rows of prayer flags floating in front of the green and red columns, and the thousands of butter lamps in the hall are shining with light red flames. This is a pure world with solemn yet gorgeous decorations. The infinite Buddhist ideas are shining through the past and the present, and devout believers worship the ancient temple, knock on the long-closed door, and try to find spiritual comfort in the Buddhist world.

17 拉卜楞寺
Labrang Monastery

拉卜楞寺是藏传佛教格鲁派的六大寺之一，全世界著名的藏传佛教学院之一，拥有非常完整的藏传佛教教学体系。寺庙的建筑风格承袭藏传佛教的热烈与庄严，带着历史的烟尘和满身的金碧辉煌，屹立在广袤的甘南草原上。

　　拉卜楞寺透亮的青石路面、斑驳的墙面、随风舞动的经幡、僧人的朗朗诵经声……穿行其间，仿佛是在虚无与现实之间穿梭行走。拉卜楞寺超长的转经长廊共有两千余个转经筒，世所罕见。经轮长转有缘者，梵音不灭信徒心。转经筒在虔诚信徒散发着酥油馨香的手指拨动下飞转，传递着信徒与佛菩萨间的沟通，为无数行者净化心灵，也记录着众生的孤独和虔诚。

　　Labrang Monastery is one of the six temples of the Gelug Sect of Zang Buddhism. It is one of the most famous Zang Buddhist school in the world and has a very complete Zang Buddhist teaching system in China. The temple's architectural style inherits the warmth and solemnity of Zang Buddhism, standing on the vast Gannan Grassland with historical traces and glories.

　　Walking through the shining bluestone pavement, mottled walls, waving prayer flags, and chanting in Labrang Monastery…seems to be walking between nothingness and reality. There is a super long prayer corridor of more than 2,000 prayer wheels in Labrang Monastery, which is rare in the world. For those who are predestined to revolve the prayer wheel, the Sanskrit will long live in their hearts. The prayer wheel is rolling by the fingers of the devout believers exuding the scent of butter, conveying the communication between the believer and the Buddha and Bodhisattva, purifying the hearts of countless practitioners, and also recording the loneliness and piety of sentient beings.

18 仙峰寺
Xianfeng Temple

仙峰寺因旁靠峨眉山仙峰岩而得名，宋、元时为小庙，明万历年间扩建并改名，后毁于火灾，现存建筑物是清乾隆时泰安和尚重建的，是峨眉山八大寺庙之一。

仙峰寺闲隐在峨眉山中，深藏于层峦叠嶂之处，临着烟树云海，远眺奇峰险壑。寺前古木参天，寺后长寿岩高插入云，恰似神仙出没的地方。悠久的古刹濡染着灵山秀水，亦有着淡然闲逸的风雅；那缥缈绝俗的香火，浸洗着思想的源泉。在万象的苍茫中蜕去一身肉骨凡胎，以恬淡的心走进仙峰寺，走进古刹千年的禅境里。

The Xianfeng Temple is named after the nearby Xianfeng Rock of Mount Emei. It was a small temple during the Song and Yuan dynasties and then was expanded and renamed during the Wanli period of the Ming Dynasty. However, the present temple was rebuilt in the Qianlong Period of the Qing Dynasty by the Monk Tai'an because the original temple was destroyed in a fire. The temple is one of the eight famous temples on Mount Emei.

Hidden in Mount Emei, Xianfeng Temple is located deep in the ridges of forests, facing the sea of lush trees and clouds, overlooking the strange peaks and dangerous valleys. The ancient trees in front of the temple are towering to the sky, and Longevity Rock behind the temple is high into the clouds, what a paradise on earth. The long-standing ancient temple is colored with beautiful mountains and rivers, and also has a cool and leisurely elegance. The ethereal incense is soaking the source of thought. Walking into the Zen world created by the ancient temple, you will forget about your body just holding a pure heart.

19 万年寺
Wannian Temple

万年寺始建于东晋，相传为汉代采药老人蒲公礼佛处，是峨眉山历史最悠久的古刹。寺庙原有殿宇七重，规模宏大，几经兴废，现今只剩一座明代无梁砖殿。

　　万年寺建在群山之中凸起的一座山峰上，诸峰相映，苍翠环绕。放眼看去，飞檐斗拱辉映日月，碧瓦精舍光耀云天，情韵流畅且气象完整。寺中环境清幽，留存有大量历史碑刻，其中最著名的是宋代书法家米芾手书的"第一山碑"。在寺中细数那些云烟过往，与古木山泉为邻，与清风流云为伴，参悟禅意，心中自成一方清雅之境。

　　The Wannian Temple was built in the Eastern Jin Dynasty. According to legend, it was the place where Pu Gong, the old gatherer of herbs, paying respect to Buddha in the Han Dynasty. It is the oldest ancient temple on Mount Emei. The temple originally had a large scale with seven halls. After several rises and falls, there is only one beamless brick hall built in the Ming Dynasty left.

　　The Wannian Temple was built on a raised peak among the mountains and surrounded by peaks and green trees. The temple is in a smooth sentiment and complete tenderness with flying eaves and arches, green tiles, and shining walls. The environment of the temple is quiet and there are a large number of historical monuments, the most famous of which is the "First Mountain Monument" handwritten by Mi Fu, the calligrapher in the Song Dynasty. Counting the stories of the past, living next to the ancient woods, mountains, and springs, and accompanied by the clear breeze and flowing clouds in the temple, one can understand the Zen and have a peaceful and elegant state of mind.

20 潭柘寺
Tanzhe Temple

潭柘寺始建于西晋,距今已有一千七百多年历史,是北京最古老的寺庙,素有"先有潭柘寺,后有北京城"的说法。潭柘寺香火鼎盛,明清两代发展成为皇家寺院,自有一番磅礴气象。

寺内古树参天,佛塔林立,红墙碧瓦的殿宇亭榭依山而筑。在潭柘寺中,鸟语溪声断续,山光云影玲珑,可以看千峰拱翠万壑堆云,听晨钟暮鼓飞泉夜雨,望雄峰捧日层峦架月,观御亭流杯锦屏雪浪。佛堂幽寂禅声动,总有绝妙梵音留驻人心,烦恼、愚痴、渴求、贪欲和嗔恨,似乎都能够在此获得解脱。

The Tanzhe Temple was built in the Western Jin Dynasty and has a history of more than 1,700 years. It is the oldest temple in Beijing and there is a statement of "Beijing city was built after the founding of Tanzhe Temple". Tanzhe Temple was prosperous with many visitors, especially during the Ming and Qing dynasties when it became a royal temple.

The temple is built along the ridges of the mountain with towering ancient trees, numerous pagodas, and the hall and pavilions in red walls and blue tiles. In the Tanzhe temple, one can hear the birds singing and streams running, watch the exquisite mountains and clouds, and enjoy the famous views in the temple. With the silent meditation in the Buddhist halls and wonderful sanskrit sound lingering in the heart, it seems that worries, ignorance, craving, greed, and hatred can all be relived here.

第五章
Chapter 5

道法自然
Following Rules of the Nature

一、著名道观
Famous Taoist temples

01 东岳庙
Dongyue Temple

东岳信仰是中国古老的信仰之一，与国家政治制度有着较为密切的联系，元代帝王就在当时世界闻名的国际化大都市——元大都（今北京）建立了东岳庙。随着世俗王权的巩固与元大都城市文化的繁荣发展，东岳庙香火逐渐旺盛。熙来攘往的人流，定期举办的各类宗教活动，还有热闹繁华的庙会，东岳庙在不知不觉间变成了一个热闹欢乐的公共空间。

几百年来，东岳庙会一直是北京城中重要的人文景观。如今的东岳庙将这段与北京城不可分割的人文历史浓缩于庙中，成为了一座展示北京城生活变化的民俗博物馆，等待着有心的人们去探寻这个城市的记忆。

Worship of Dongyue Mount Taishan is one of the beliefs in ancient China, which is closely related to the national political system. Emperors of the Yuan Dynasty built Donyue Temple in the Great Capital of Yuan (now Beijing), a world-famous international metropolis. With the consolidation of monarchy and the development and prosperity of urban culture in the Great Capital of Yuan, many believers went to worship in Dongyue Temple. Streams of people coming and going in different religious activities held regularly and lively and to prosperous temple fair, Dongyue Temple was unconsciously turned into a bustling and pleasant public place.

For centuries, Dongyue Temple has always been a significant cultural landscape in the history of Beijing. Nowadays, its culture and history inseparable from Beijing City are embodied in the temple and turn it into a folklore museum to display changes in life in Beijing, waiting for visitors to explore the memory of this city with interest.

02 白云观
Baiyun Taoist Temple

　　白云观位于北京西城区西便门外，前身系唐代的天长观，明代易名为白云观，是道教全真派发祥地之一。

　　中国的古寺多在名山大川，而白云观却身处闹市之中。自明清以来，北京城春节期间一大乐事就是去白云观参加庙会，拜本命神、摸石猴、打金钱眼，还有庙会上琳琅满目的杂货小吃，构成了北京古城几百年来社会风俗的经典场景。岁月将中国古老的信仰与多样的文化熔铸于一体，深深植根于人们的心灵，并将继续影响着这个城市人们的精神文化生活。

　　Baiyun Taoist Temple is outside the Xibianmen Gate in Xicheng District, Beijing. It was originally named Tianchang Taoist Temple in the Tang Dynasty and was renamed Baiyun Taoist Temple in the Ming Dynasty. The temple is one of the three cradles of Quanzhen Taoism.

　　Ancient temples of China are mostly scattered in well-known mountains or by famous rivers. Since the Ming and Qing dynasties, one of the joys in Beijing during the Spring Festival is to visit the Baiyun Taoist Temple Fair. You may worship the God of your animal zodiac, touch the stone monkey, throw a coin to hit the clock in the central hole of a large coin, and go shopping among various commodities and snacks, and all these illustrate a classic scene of social customs in ancient Beijing city for centuries. Time has integrated ancient religions and diversified cultures of China, making them rooted in the mind of people and continuously influencing the spirit and cultural life of residents in this city.

# 永乐宫
Yongle Palace

永乐宫原名"大纯万寿宫",因故址在山西省芮城县永乐镇而改称永乐宫。永乐宫观内沿中轴线兴建龙虎殿、三清殿、纯阳殿和重阳殿等建筑,并且自前至后殿宇规模和间距,依次减小。寺内建筑高耸云霄,画栋雕梁;周围布有参天古柏,颇有"道院森森,殿阁巍巍"的肃穆气氛。

永乐宫是中国现存最大、保存最为完整的道教宫观。永乐宫以精美绝伦的壁画艺术、富丽堂皇的宫廷建筑,以及独具特色的道教文化享誉华夏、名扬四海。永乐宫中九百六十平方米的精美壁画,至今为东西方艺术家所赞赏和膜拜,并因此被誉为"世界超级艺术"。其中《朝元图》是元代壁画艺术的最高典范。

Originally called "The Grand Chunyang Wanshou Palace", Yongle Palace was renamed since it was located in Yongle Town, Ruicheng County, Shanxi Province. Longhu Temple, Sanqing Temple, Chunyang Temple, and Chongyang Temple are built along the medial axis of Yongle Palace, where the scales and distances in between are sequentially decreased to the back. Richly ornamented architecture in the palace soar into the sky with towering cypresses around, creating a solemn atmosphere of "quiet Taoist temples and towering palaces".

Yongle Palace is the best preserved and the largest remaining Taoist temple, which is famous at home and abroad for its exquisite frescos, splendid palaces, and unique Taoist culture. The 960 square meter exquisite fresco in Yongle Palace has been appreciated and admired by artists in the east and west and is named "The Super Art in the World", where the painting "Paying Homage to the Primeval Lord of Heaven" is the best example of fresco art in Yuan Dynasty."

04 中岳庙
Zhongyue Temple

中岳庙位于河南省登封市嵩山东麓，始建于秦，原为太室祠。它是一座充分体现中国古代传统礼制观念的建筑群，尊卑有序、等级分明的特点在几百个的殿、亭、宫、阁、楼、台、廊庑间被体现得淋漓尽致。在礼制观念的主导下，主体建筑的宫楼殿宇宏大壮丽，而附属建筑的廊庑则素雅质朴，体现了尊卑有序的价值观念，也从建筑的视觉效果上体现了中国古代先人的审美追求。既要有庄重宏大的对称均衡美，也要有主次鲜明的层次美，"美"与"礼"在古庙中形成了完美的统一。

古庙被翠树烟岚的嵩山环抱，紧邻千年古刹少林寺，亦不免受其影响，许多佛教元素也融入其间，形成了中岳庙儒释道交融的文化特征。

Located at the east foot of Songshan Mountain, Dengfeng City, Henan Province, Zhongyue Temple was built in the Qin Dynasty and it was originally the Taishi Temple to worship the God of Taishi Mountain. The architectural complex embodies the traditional ritual idea in ancient China, where hierarchy and order are fully expressed by hundreds of temples, halls, palaces, pavilions, buildings, terraces, and corridors. Guided by the ritual idea, the main buildings are magnificent, while corridors of subsidiary buildings are plain and elegant, reflecting the values of order and aesthetic pursuit of Chinese ancestors in visual effect. There is both beauty of magnificence and symmetry and that of hierarchical layers. "Beauty" and "Rituals" are perfectly integrated into the ancient temple.

Embraced by fog and green trees in Songshan Mountain and near Shaolin Temple, a temple over one thousand years, the Taoist temple is inevitably influenced by it and absorbs some Buddhist elements to take on a cultural characteristic of combining Confucianism, Buddhism, and Taoism.

崂山太清宫
Taiqing Palace in Laoshan Mountain

　　崂山太清宫位于海滨名城青岛，始建于西汉，后屡加修建，现存建筑主要为明代遗迹。崂山道教历史悠久，且因其隐逸文化而独树一帜，"崂山道士"遂成了中国传统文化语境下的世外高人。

　　崂山太清宫所在地海阔山高，气候温和，名木奇花更胜江南。如此清净无垢之地，吸引了历朝历代豪杰名士隐遁于此。他们每日清修赏花，寄情山水林泉，留下了许多千古传颂的诗歌辞赋。诗仙李白曾有过于"崂山餐紫霞"的浪漫畅想，文豪苏东坡也留下了"崂山多隐君子，可闻而不可见"的感慨。

　　经年累月，太清宫中的藤树名花、古石苔痕、诗文题刻交叠融合，恰是道教天人合一价值观的完美体现。而归隐的文豪名士与山水自然的一段缘分及其所衍生的思想与艺术也随着海树山花融入了中华文化的血脉。

　　Located in the famous coastal city Qingdao, Taiqing Palace in Laoshan Mountain was built in the Western Han Dynasty and renovated afterward. The existing architecture is mainly the relics of the Ming Dynasty. Taoism in Laoshan Mountain has a long history and is unique for its seclusion culture. Therefore, "Laoshan Taoist priest" has been the synonym of secluded talent in the traditional Chinese cultural context.

　　Taiqing Palace in Laoshan Mountain is on a high hill by the broad sea, where the climate is mild and precious trees and flowers are even more beautiful than those in southern China. Such a peaceful and quiet place attracted heroes and literati in different dynasties to live in seclusion here. They conduct spiritual practice, admire the beauty of flowers and express their feelings through mountains, rivers, forests, and springs, leaving poems and odes handed down from one generation to another. Fairy poet Li Bai had the romantic imagination of "Appreciating glowing light in Laoshan Mountain". The great lyric poet Su Dongpo also wrote: "Many hermits live in the Laoshan Mountain, I have heard of them but never meet any."

　　With the passing of time, vine trees, flowers, stones, moss, and inscribed poems in Taiqing Palace mingled with each other, perfectly reflecting the theory of Taoism that man is an integral part of nature. The tie between Secluded literati and celebrities and the nature and the thoughts and art yielded are also integrated into Chinese culture with sea, trees, mountains, and flowers.

青羊宫
Qingyang Palace

　　青羊宫位于四川省成都市,据传始建于西周,古时初名"青羊肆"。青羊宫祭祀三清尊神和老子、玉皇大帝,也祭祀唐代帝王李渊、李世民父子。青羊宫的建筑整体简洁庄重,但在细节装饰上却一派繁丽精巧,到处是精美的雕刻与彩绘。装饰题材丰富,大多是反映道教中吉祥如意、长生不老、羽化成仙的内容。宫观内环境清幽,钟声悠扬,亭台殿宇中满是历代遗迹珍存。

　　青羊宫虽是清修之所,却身处闹市,不但有传统的庙会日,还有历史悠久的"花会"日,每逢节会,宫内香烟缭绕,钟磬悠悠,人潮熙攘,热闹非凡。古时这里是市民城市生活的重要组成部分,是传统城市居民精神生活与社会活动的重要场所。于是许多关于巴蜀、关于老成都的记忆和民俗都在青羊宫的袅袅香烟中飘进人们的心中久久不肯散去。

Qingyang Palace is in Chengdu City, Sichuan Province. It is said that Qingyang Palace was built in the Western Zhou Dynasty and was originally named "Qingyang Temple". It is a place to worship Sanqing God, and Li Yuan and Li Shimin, two emperors in the Tang Dynasty. The architecture of Qingyang Palace is simple and solemn. However, their ornaments are elaborate and exquisite with delicate sculptures and colored paintings. The ornaments are rich in themes, most of them reflecting auspiciousness, immortality, and immortalization in Taoism. The palace is peaceful and quiet with bell tolls. Relics and precious collections are displayed in temples, halls, terraces, and palaces.

As Qingyang Palace is situated in the downtown area, it is a place not only for spiritual practice, but also for holding traditional temple fairs and flower fairs. Whenever there is a fair or festival, Qingyang Palace is lively, full of incense smoke with bell tolls, chimes, and surging crowds. In ancient times, it is an important part of the lives of residents, being a vital area for the spiritual and social lives of traditional urban residents. Therefore, with the incense smoke in Qingyang Palace, memory and folk customs of the Sichuan area and ancient Chengdu were engraved on the minds of many people.

07 紫霄宫
Purple Heaven Palace

紫霄宫始建于北宋宣和年间，位于湖北武当山展旗峰之下，是武当山保存较完整的皇家庙观建筑群，具有神圣威严的皇家风范。

"紫霄"在道教意义中代表着至高极大，也代表着众星之主，更代表着仙境美景。因此，紫霄宫凭借山势的壮丽险峻，巧妙地采取逐级抬升的手法，精心布局了朝拜殿、龙虎殿、紫霄大殿之间的高差层次。神宫琳宇云端高峙、庄严肃穆，使得朝圣进香者必须仰首而视，顿生顶礼膜拜之心。

紫霄宫内装饰考究，建筑、雕刻、彩绘皆是皇室形制。紫霄宫高耸宏大之余，也不乏池、渠、桥、井等景观小品，尤其将天然水脉引入人工雕造的园林小景，使人文建筑与自然山水融为一体，更好地体现出了道教中"天人合一"的理念。

Purple Heaven Palace was built in the Xuanhe period (1119-1125) of the Northern Song Dynasty. It is at the foot of Zhanqi Peak of Wudang Mountain, Hubei Province. As a well-preserved royal temple architectural complex in Wudang Mountain, it is in holy and solemn royal majesty.

Purple Heaven means supremacy, lord of stars, and fairyland in Taoism. Taking advantage of the steepness and magnificence of the mountain, Worship Hall, Dragon and Tiger Hall, and Great Purple Heaven Hall are configured ingeniously in different altitudes and levels by uplifting grade by grade. Halls and palaces are towering in clouds, solemn and decent, making worshippers admire them since they have to raise their heads to appreciate.

Ornaments in Purple Heaven Palace, including interior architecture, sculptures, and colored paintings are all tailored following the royal hierarchical system. Towering and magnificent, Purple Heaven Palace also has landscapes such as ponds, ditches, bridges, and wells. Water from nature is brought into garden landscapes to integrate the cultural architecture and mountains and rivers in nature, better reflecting the theory that "man is an integral part of nature" in Taoism.

茅山道院
Maoshan Taoist Temples

　　茅山位于江苏句容东南，早在秦代已有人于此地炼丹修行，隋唐时大建宫观，至宋而极盛。那时的茅山，宫观道院、精舍茅庵极多，高人辈出，羽流云集，备受皇室推崇。

　　抗日战争期间，茅山道教宫观庙宇多遭焚毁，仅存九霄、元符、崇禧三宫与德佑、仁佑、乾元、玉晨、白云五观，时称"三宫五观"。1949年后，原来的三宫五观合并为"茅山道院"。茅山道院中的九霄万福宫坐落于大茅峰之顶，为茅山道院之首，始建于汉代，现存宋元明清历朝遗珍，尤其是雕刻泥塑最为精美。茅山道院历史悠久，其斋醮法事活动尤具特色，千载之间绵延不衰，是中国为数不多活态传承的道教宗教仪式。仪式中的唱诵技巧、曲牌名目更是中国古代音乐的珍贵资料。

Maoshan Mountain is in the southeast of Jurong City, Jiangsu Province. As early as in the Qin Dynasty, some Taoist priests made pills of immorality and conducted spiritual practice here. Temples and palaces were built here in the Tang Dynasty and local Taoism reached its peak in the Song Dynasty. At that time, there were many temples, palaces, and viharas in Maoshan Mountain, attracting Taoist priests to gather here, among which there are lots of eminent ones, and Taoism was highly regarded by royal families.

During the War of Resistance Against Japanese Aggression, most Taoist temples and palaces in Maoshan Mountain were burnt down, leaving only Jiuxiao Palace, Yuanfu Palace, Chongxi Palace, Deyou Temple, Renyou Temple, Qianyuan Temple, Yuchen Temple, and Baiyun Temple, called "Three Palaces and Five Temples". After 1949, these three palaces and five temples are integrated into the "Maoshan Taoist Temples". Among them, Jiuxiao Wanfu Palace is located on top of Damao Peak. As the top palace among Maoshan Taoist Temples, Jiuxiao Wanfu Palace was built in the Han Dynasty and it preserves heritage and relics from Song, Yuan, Ming and Qing dynasties, with wooden and clay sculptures most exquisite. With a long history, the Maoshan Taoist Temples are unique in their rites, which are handed down through thousands of years as one of the few dynamically inherited Taoist rites. The chanting techniques and tune names are precious materials of ancient Chinese music.

09 抱朴道院
Baopu Taoist Temple

在杭州西湖北岸的葛岭山上，隐匿着一座千年古观——抱朴道院。古观初名抱朴庐，始建于晋，至元毁于兵火，明初重建。古观建筑飞檐翘角，古迹众多、楹联满目，一望便知在一千七百余载的岁月磨砺下，魏晋风骨的余脉与江南旖旎的风情交融，将古观塑造成一处极清静悠然之地。不然以西湖美景繁盛之地，何以藏起这一方清幽之所。

据传，长于艺术赏鉴的南宋权臣贾似道曾将此观占为一己之别墅。沿着道院石阶缓缓而上，蓦然回首时已将烟波浩渺的西湖尽收眼底。独坐于苔痕斑驳、碧草葱茏的林泉边，品茶沉思，不远处巍峨殿宇中篆烟缭绕，不知不觉间忘却了自己，也忘却了凡尘。

Baopu Taoist Temple, a Taoist temple of over a thousand years is located in Geling Mountain on the northern bank of the West Lake in Hangzhou City. Originally named Baopu Cottage, the temple was built in the Jin Dynasty, burnt down in wars in the Yuan Dynasty, and rebuilt in the early Ming Dynasty. The ancient temple with cornices has many relics and couplets. Take a look at it, and you will know the temple has been shaped into a peaceful and quiet place with both spirit in the Wei and Jin dynasties and lovely scenes south of the Yangtze River over 1700 years. Otherwise, how can such a quiet and secluded temple be concealed near the West Lake, a place of beautiful landscapes and prosperity?

It is said that Jia Sidao, a powerful official and good connoisseur in the Southern Song Dynasty had occupied the temple and taken it as his mansion. Go up along the stone stairs of the temple, and you can have a panoramic view of the expanse and misty West Lake when you look around. In a thriving forest, sitting alone by the river on a grassland dotted with moss, tasting the tea while thinking, looking at the smoke in towering temples and palaces, and you will unconsciously forget yourself and the world.

太和宫
Taihe Palace

太和宫又称大岳太和宫,位于湖北省武当山主峰——天柱峰的绝顶之上,众峰拱托,极目四方,显现出一种独步云天的气魄。太和宫依居天险、随山就势,肃穆庄严、大气磅礴,正所谓"千层楼阁空中起,万叠云山足下环"。

太和宫主要有金殿、皇经堂、紫金城、朝拜殿等古代建筑。以金顶围墙为界,墙外称"太和宫",墙里叫"紫金城"。"北有紫禁城,南有紫金城",可见当时太和宫的地位之高。紫金城的城墙上有东西南北四座天门,四座天门临空云上,彰显天庭仙界的威严。皇经堂的隔扇门上浮雕着珍禽异兽和道教神仙故事,内有铸造和雕刻工艺的灿烂瑰宝——琳琅满目的神像、法器。太和宫是武当山的最高胜境,漫步云端,感受惊心动魄的震撼,虔诚之心油然而生。

Taihe Palace, also called Dayue Taihe Palace, is located on top of Tianzhu Peak, the main peak of Wudang Mountain, Hubei Province. It overlooks other peaks and looks around as far as the eye can see as if it were the only temple in heaven. Taihe Palace takes advantage of steepness and is built according to the mountainous terrain. Solemn and magnificent, the temple is described as "The multistory building is in the air with clouds curved at foot of it".

Taihe Palace is mainly composed of ancient buildings such as Golden Temple, Huangjing Hall, Zijin City and Worship Hall. Taking the golden-ceiling enclosing wall as the boundary, the part outside it is called "Taihe Palace" and the inside part is called "Zijin City". It is said that "There is a Zijin City (the Forbidden City) in the north, and a Zijin City in the south (note: two places are pronounced the same but written in different Chinese characters)", from which we could see the important status of Taihe Palace at that time. In the wall of Zijin City, there are four celestial gates in the north, south, east, and west over the clouds to show the dignity of heaven. Precious animals and birds and Taoist stories are embossed on partition doors of Huangjing Hall, in which there are various statues of Gods and Taoist instruments, presenting the splendid casting and carving techniques. Taihe Palace is the top landscape of Wudang Mountain. If you walk in clouds to feel the shock in the temple, the pious feeling will arise spontaneously.

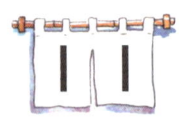

天后宫
Tianhou Temple

  天后宫亦称天妃宫，俗称娘娘庙，始建于元朝，位于天津市古文化街，是中国现存年代最早的妈祖庙之一。天后宫坐西朝东，面向海河，有戏楼、幡杆、山门、牌坊、前殿、大殿、藏经阁、启圣祠等建筑。大殿是天后宫的主体建筑，具有典型的明代中晚期木结构建筑风格。前殿有护法神——王灵官、千里眼、顺风耳等。正殿神龛里的海神天后，慈眉善目，仪态端庄。左右立着四个彩衣侍女，其中两人手执长柄扇，另两人分别捧着宝瓶和印绶。天后宫的神灵崇拜广泛，亦有天津当地的民间信仰，如王三奶奶、白老太太、挑水哥哥、马王爷等。几百年来，天后宫香火不断，前来祈福的善男信女络绎不绝。

Tianhou Temple, also named Tianfei Temple, is commonly called Goddess Temple. Located in Tianjin Ancient Culture Street, it was built in the Yuan Dynasty and is one of the earliest existing Mazu Temple. Sitting in the west and facing the east, the temple is open towards Haihe River with a theater stage, prayer flag rod, a gate to the temple, memorial archway, front hall, main hall, depositary of Taoist texts, and Qisheng Temple. The main hall is the major architecture of Tianhou Temple in a typical wooden architectural style of the middle and late Ming Dynasty. There are guardian gods in the front hall: Immortal official Wang, Thousand-mile Eye, Wind-accompany Ear, and so on. Mazu is in the niche of the main hall, merciful and dignified. Four maids are standing on the left and right of her, and two of them are holding long-handled fans while the other two holding a vase and a seal respectively. Many gods are worshipped in Tianhou Temple, even including local gods in Tianjin, such as Granny Wangsan, Granny Bai, Brother Water-carrier, God Ma, and so on. For centuries, Tianhou Temple has been worshipped by an endless stream of pilgrims.

真武阁
Zhenwu Taoist Temple

真武阁始建于明代，位于广西容县城东绣江北岸。古时容县多火灾，时人疑为南山火怪作祟，故建真武阁以供奉北方水神——真武帝君，起到镇压火怪的作用。

真武阁坐北朝南，为三层木结构建筑楼阁，但屋檐挑出很大而柱高甚低，因此看上去它不像是一座三层建筑，更像是一座有三重屋檐的单层建筑，舒展大气，飘逸灵动。它建于沙堆之上，无巨石为基，楼梯又仅是木构榫卯结构，无钢铁固定。历经四百多年，真武阁虽经受了多次地震和风暴的袭扰，但仍岿然耸立，可见其营造结构之高妙，被建筑学家梁思成称为"我国古代建筑史上罕见的一颗明珠"。

Located on the northern bank of Xiujiang River in the east of Rongxian County, Guangxi Zhuang Autonomous Region, Zhenwu Taoist Temple was built in the Ming Dynasty. In ancient times, fires broke out frequently in Rongxian County and people doubted they were caused by the fire monster in Nanshan Mountain. Therefore, Zhenwu Taoist Temple enshrines God of Water in the north, God Zhenwu, to suppress the fire monster.

Sitting in the north and facing the south, Zhenwu Taoist Temple is a three-tier wooden building. However, its eaves are protruding but the height of columns is short. Therefore, it doesn't look like a three-tier building but a one-tier building with three layers of eaves, which is stretching, magnificent, elegant, and flexible. Built on sand piles, it has no large stone base and its stairs are installed through wooden tenon and mortise joints structure without using any steel nails. Zhenwu Taoist Temple withstood earthquakes and storms for over 400 years and we can see how wonderful the structure is. It was hailed as "A rare pearl in the ancient architectural history of China" by Liang Sicheng, a famous architect in China.

泰山岱庙
Taishan Dai Temple

　　岱庙位于山东省泰安市泰山脚下，始建于汉。岱庙虽被称作庙，但又不同于一般的庙宇。这里是历代帝王祭祀泰山神灵、举行祭天大典的场所。因是皇家祭祀，其建筑形制为城堞高筑的宫殿式样，巍峨雄伟。古庙布局宏大有序，如宫殿一般分中、东、西三路，共九进院落。中轴线上依次坐落着功能礼制不同的诸多建筑。

　　岱庙虽是道家宫观，却深深融入了儒家色彩。中华文明自古"国之大事，在祀与戎"，因此岱庙中最重要的建筑是建于宋代的天贶殿，其营造规格为中国古代建筑最高级别，而殿内的壁画更是中国古代壁画中的绝世珍品。

Located at the foot of Mount Taishan, Tai'an City, Shandong Province, Dai Temple was built in the Han Dynasty. Being called a temple, it is different from general temples, since it is the place for successive emperors to worship Mount Taishan and heaven. As for royal religious activities, the parapet is built high under royal palace style, making the temple magnificent and lofty. The ancient temple is grand and orderly, divided into the middle, eastern and western parts and 9 courtyards. Along the medial axis, there are various buildings with different functions following different standards of the ritual system.

Although Dai Temple is a Taoist temple, it is greatly influenced by Confucianism. For Chinese civilization, "Two missions are the most important for a country: worship and war." Therefore, the most essential architecture in Dai Temple is Tiankuang Temple, which was built in the Song Dynasty. Its construction standards are the highest among ancient Chinese architecture, while frescos in the temple are treasures in ancient Chinese fresco art.

14 晋祠
Jin Temple

晋祠位于太原市区西南，始建于北魏，是为纪念周武王次子姬虞而建的。晋祠园林秀美、古建精绝、彩塑灵动，无一不是当世国宝。近百座殿堂楼阁、亭台桥榭集宋至清历代建筑之精华，其中翘楚当数北宋修建的圣母殿。殿堂出檐深远、宽大疏朗，充满皇家宫苑的雄浑气势。殿内有四十三尊宋代侍女彩塑，它们形象逼真，情态灵动，举手投足间大宋的风雅仪态丝毫毕现。殿前的鱼沼飞梁更是中国古代桥梁建筑中仅存的十字桥孤例。还有通透轻盈的真趣亭，小巧别致的流碧榭，庄严神圣的舍利塔，古老清澈的难老泉……自然山水与人文建筑相结合，营建出"山西小江南"的千古名胜。

自然造化与历代遗珍的完美结合造就了流传千载的建筑园林、雕塑碑刻，也传承了宗教祭祀、龙狮图腾等文化内涵。晋祠不是一座普通意义上的古老祠堂，更是一座融建筑、雕塑、园林于一体的艺术圣殿与博物馆，以其丰厚独特的历史文化遗产静待人们寻访。

Located southwest of Taiyuan City, Jin Temple was built in the Northern Wei Dynasty in memory of Ji Yu, the second son of King Wu of the Zhou Dynasty. The whole temple can be seen as a national treasure with its elegant garden, exquisite ancient architecture, and lively painted sculptures. Nearly a hundred palaces, buildings, pavilions, terraces, and bridges reflect the essences of architecture from the Song Dynasty to the Qing Dynasty, where the best building is Shengmu Temple constructed in the Northern Song Dynasty. Its eaves are protruding, wide and spacious, full of the magnificence of imperial palaces. There are 43 statues of maids of the Song Dynasty, and they look vivid and lively, revealing the elegance of the Song Dynasty in their gestures. The flying bridge across the fish pond is the only remaining example of the cross-bridge in ancient Chinese bridge structure. Moreover, there is ventilated and light Zhenqu Pavilion, a small and unconventional Liubi Water Pavilion, solemn and holy Stupa, and old and clean Nanlao Spring … The natural landscape is combined with cultural architecture to create a place of interest over thousands of years as the "southern landscape in Shanxi Province".

The perfect combination of nature and heritage from dynasties not only creates architecture, gardens, sculpture, and inscription that are handed down through generations but also inherits cultural connotations of religious rites and totems like dragons and lions. Jin Temple is not only an ancient memorial temple in the general sense, but also an art temple and a museum combining architecture, sculpture, and garden, which is there to be visited with rich and unique historical and cultural heritage.

15 临水宫
Linshui Palace

　　临水宫位于福建省古田县，建于山坡之上，是一座充满道教风格的宫庙建筑。据传它始建于唐代，供奉着临水夫人陈靖姑，是世界各地临水宫的祖庭。临水宫历代多有修缮，保存了福建地区不同历史时期的装饰艺术、民俗风情，以及本地民间传统技艺，如石雕、灰塑等。因是皇封敕赐的古代宫观建筑，临水宫建筑群中最具特色的是各建筑顶部代表不同社会等级的屋顶及不同高度的翘角。屋檐的四角俱是飞扬向上，极致者卷曲反曲，具有浓郁的福建地域风格。临水宫屋脊上以灰塑技艺塑造出动物、花卉、器物等，既丰富了建筑的装饰与造型，也强化了宗教氛围，更凝聚了本地乡民千载的信仰。

Linshui Palace, an architecture in Taoist style, is built on a hillside in Gutian County, Fujian Province. It is said that the palace was built in the Tang Dynasty to worship Chen Jinggu, Madame Linshui, and it was the cradle of Linshui temples all over the world. Through many renovations, it preserves decorative art, folk customs, and traditional folk craftsmanship such as stone carving, lime sculpture, and so on. Since it is a Taoist temple rewarded by the emperor, Linshui Palace architectural complex is featured by curled corners in different heights representing different hierarchies on top of buildings. Four corners of the eave are all pointing upwards, some even curl or curl back as often seen in the local decorative style of Fujian Province. On ridges of a roof, animals, flowers, artifacts are made with lime sculpture techniques, improving decoration and portraying of the architecture but also enhancing the religious atmosphere and condensing the belief of residents over a thousand years.

Ancient Chinese Temples

Written by Guan Wei and Huixin

Illustrated by Yin Ming

First English Edition 2023

By China Pictorial Press Co., Ltd.

CHINA INTERNATIONAL COMMUNICATIONS GROUP

Copyright © China Pictorial Press Co., Ltd.

All rights reserved.

No part of this publication may be reproduced, stored in a retrieval system, or transmitted in any form or by any means, electronic, mechanical, photocopying, recording, or otherwise, without the prior written permission of China Pictorial Press Co., Ltd., except for the inclusion of brief quotations in an acknowledged review.

Address: 33 Chegongzhuang Xilu, Haidian District, Beijing, 100048, China

ISBN 978-7-5146-2068-9